HERMENEUTICS
IN ROMANS

HERMENEUTICS
IN ROMANS

PAUL'S APPROACH TO READING THE BIBLE

TRANSLATED BY: BROR ERICKSON, WESLIE ODOM, AND KRISTINA ODOM

DR. TIMO LAATO

Hermeneutics in Romans: Paul's Approach to Reading the Bible

Published by:
1517 Publishing
PO Box 54032
Irvine, CA 92619-4032

Publisher's Cataloging-In-Publication Data
(Prepared by The Donohue Group, Inc.)

Names: Laato, Timo, 1963– author. | Erickson, Bror, writer of supplementary textual content, translator, editor. | Odom, Weslie, 1982– translator. | Odom, Kristina, 1977– translator.
Title: Hermeneutics in Romans : Paul's approach to reading the Bible / Dr. Timo Laato ; translated by Bror Erickson, Weslie Odom, and Kristina Odom ; [edited and with a foreword by Bror Erickson].
Other Titles: Romarbrevets hermeneutik. English
Description: [Expanded edition]. | Irvine, CA : 1517 Publishing, [2021] | Translated from Swedish, this is an expanded version of: Romarbrevets hermeneutik. Göteborg : Församlingsförlaget, 2006. | Includes bibliographical references.
Identifiers: ISBN 9781948969314 (hardcover) | ISBN 9781948969321 (softcover) | ISBN 9781948969338 (ebook)
Subjects: LCSH: Bible. Romans—Hermeneutics. | Bible—Criticism, interpretation, etc. | Paul, the Apostle, Saint—Religion.
Classification: LCC BS2665.52 .L3313 2021 (print) | LCC BS2665.52 (ebook) | DDC 227/.1066—dc23

Printed in the United States of America

Cover art by Brenton Clarke Little

Contents

Acknowledgments

This book is an expanded version of the Swedish original, *Romarbrevets hermeneutik: En lärobok för teologer om vetenskaplig metod*, Församlingsfakultetens skriftserie nr 7, Göteborg, 2006. The first draft was presented at the North European Luther Academy symposium in Helsinki (September 1999), thereafter at the European Theological Students' Conference in Mittersill (August 2001), and finally, in connection with my teaching at the Lutheran School of Theology in Gothenburg. See my articles "Romarbrevets hermeneutiska princip" in *Anden och Ordet*, Kungälv, 2000, 17–39; and later, "Romans as the Completion of Bonhoeffer's Hermeneutics," in *JETS* 58 (2015), 709–29. The Swedish original has been translated also into Russian: Герменевтика Послания к Римлянам: Руководство по научному методу для теологов, Vitebsk, 2015. A short summary of the results, presented in this book, has been published in Norwegian ("Kristus—Skriftens kjerne og stjerne," in *Guds ord: Det är vårt arvegods—en artikkelsamling om skrifsynet og reformasjonen*, ed. Konrad Fjell, Oslo, 2017, 98–114) as well as in Danish ("Kristus—Skriftens kerne og stjerne," in *Guds ord: Fundamentet for evangelisk luthersk tro*, ed. Konrad Fjell, Aarhus, 2017, 113–27). In addition, I have made use of my master's thesis in Greek philology: "Paul's Use of the Septuagint in Romans 9–11" (University of Turku, 2019). The Swedish original was translated into English by Weslie and Kristina Odom as well as Bror Erickson. After that, it has been adjusted and expanded by the author in different ways.

Translator's Foreword

I have been asked to introduce you to Dr. Timo Laato. To begin with, Timo is a close friend, colleague, and mentor. I hold his encouragement and instruction dear. His emails are opened immediately. Any project he might ask of me I embark upon knowing full well he always has something to teach me. To translate and edit this man's work has satisfied every academic itch I have. Moreover, he makes exegetical research relevant. If on the surface his work looks intimidating, a reader will soon find that he has the greatest ability to break everything down and present it in a way that is not only accessible but also exciting.

Timo is Senior Lecturer of New Testament at the Lutheran Theological Seminary in Gothenburg, Sweden. He has written extensively in German, Swedish, English, and Finnish (his mother tongue) and is well known in exegetical circles for his critiques of the so-called Finnish school of Luther studies led by Mannerma and the New Perspective on Paul. He is meticulous in his research and precise in the presentations of his arguments, yet very kind and gracious to those with whom he disagrees. Humble enough to hear; Lutheran enough to stand. *Hermeneutics in Romans* is no exception.

In this book, he offers a fresh approach to hermeneutics in which he both plans and executes an escape from the Kantian prison that Biblical research finds itself in today. He first identifies the atheistic underpinnings that hamper theological research and investigates their origins in the philosophy of Immanuel Kant. With a brief overview of twentieth-century hermeneutical approaches concentrating on the reactions of Bultmann and Barth, he picks up on hitherto ignored work by Dietrich Bonhoeffer and sees a promising new approach.

With this, he goes on the offensive in a field that has been dominated for far too long by open attacks on the veracity of Scripture. Yet Timo manages to steer clear of the naïve Biblicism and fundamentalism that unwittingly calls for a retreat from any meaningful defense of Scripture in academia or even in the general public.

Coupling the insights of Bonhoeffer with the Lutheran notion that Scripture interprets Scripture, Timo then launches into an exegetical tour through Romans, concentrating especially on chapters 9–11. He investigates how Paul himself approaches hermeneutics in his interpretation of the Old Testament with its application for the New Testament church. He then shows how Bonhoeffer's approach to hermeneutics coincides with that of Paul's own principles of Biblical interpretation and therefore commends itself to Christian believers in our own day and age.

Pr. Bror Erickson
Transfiguration Sunday, 2020

I
Introduction

The Critical Significance of Romans in the History of the Church

The Epistle to the Romans has always been remarkable in its ability to show the way forward from spiritual depravation to new revival even during the darkest hours of church history. This was true as far back as the days of Saint Augustine in his battle with Pelagius. It remained true in the sixteenth century with Martin Luther in his fight for the proper doctrine of justification. It was the case with John Wesley in his spiritual agony. It proved itself again when Karl Barth set out to conquer the nexus of the problems with liberal theology at the beginning of the twentieth century.[1]

The Epistle to the Romans seems to contain dynamite, which time after time ignites an intense process within academic theology and the church. Radical and surprising results arise. It is difficult to explain the reason for this development except to say that history truly does repeat itself! In the deepest sense, Romans presents the "last will" or "spiritual testament" of the apostle and, as such, has been diligently studied by his followers and advocates throughout the centuries. Over and over again, they have discovered something within it that has changed not only their own way of thinking and believing but also that of others around them. Then in some form, a reformation rooted in Pauline theology often follows. Consequently, the significance of Romans cannot be overestimated. Without a doubt, the argumentation of that letter is worth reading and contemplating even today.

The Church's Decisive Hour Today

Today, it is evident that churches live in the midst of a deep crisis. This time around, the crisis is called "Bible criticism," which is practiced by theological faculties around the world with the help of the so called historical-critical method. Modern exegesis itself exists in a kind of transitional period. New methods are constantly being developed, and though the traditional methods have not been abandoned, they are usually considered inadequate. Rhetorical, semiotic, narrative, and even sociological, cultural, anthropological, and psychological methodologies have emerged alongside conventional text analyses such as redaction, form, and tradition-historical criticism.[2] Indeed, the diversity in the field of exegetical research challenges everyone concerned with the biblical sources. So how should we orientate ourselves within that kind of difficult terrain?

Moreover, modern research usually finds itself at a dead end when interpreting religious texts and not allowing them to speak of a living God. Certain philosophical presuppositions (particularly Immanuel Kant's fascinating and impressive combination of rationalism and empiricism) have led many to accept that the transcendent and supernatural belong not in the realm of academic scholarship but only in the areas of aesthetics and ethics.[3] Accordingly, the occasional accusation is leveled saying that modern exegetical methods do not, in fact, further the *theological* discipline very much.[4] Against the background of such a volatile atmosphere in current research, churches seem to be in trouble with their constant talk about God. They have to work, somehow, outside of the limits of knowledge. As a result, their message is quite often marginalized to a great extent. Consequently, the crisis within Christendom becomes even more serious.

So it is once again worthwhile to study the Epistle to the Romans thoroughly. Regardless of which church body one works within, we have a mission to proclaim the epistle's message in a fresh way to parishioners at the grassroots level and others interested in hearing it. May we hope that its content will make way for a theological breakthrough and spiritual revival within Christendom today, as it has done throughout the history of the church (see above). Indeed, the reading of Romans is never in vain. Time and again it has provided new solutions to old problems. What an inspiration with regard to my work too!

Task and Approach

My purpose is to study the hermeneutics of Romans.[5] Which lines of thought does Paul follow in his understanding of the Bible—that is, the *Old* Testament? Special attention will be paid to the new theological insights that the gospel of Jesus Christ revealed to him. His way of interpreting Holy Scripture acts as a model for the theological assessment of the basis and limits of modern academic scholarship. To begin with, the task requires a brief survey of the distinctive nature of theological hermeneutics and its development so far. The overview will reveal a problematic area in hermeneutics, which serves as the starting point for my current study. Next, three different solutions will be presented in short: the hermeneutical contributions of Karl Barth, Rudolf Bultmann, and Dietrich Bonhoeffer. Unfortunately, none of these positions are completely convincing, since all require either correction or supplementation. This prompts a more careful reading of the main themes of Romans, which results in a fresh take on hermeneutics. It is then possible to explain Paul's exposition of Holy Scripture to a greater extent. Thereby, several general guidelines for his interpretation emerge. From the overall picture, focus turns to the long section of Rom. 9–11. Here Paul aims to establish Israel's place in salvation history while quoting the Old Testament more frequently than anywhere else in his letters.[6] The analysis ends with some applications of the apostolic understanding of the Bible in practice. Finally, the most significant results are summarized, and diverse conclusions are made.[7]

Hermeneutic Presuppositions

A Historical Perspective

The Hermeneutical Reorientation

Within the scope of a single presentation, it is not possible to sketch a complete line of theological development with the minutest precision starting, say, with the Age of Enlightenment (much less from the beginning). It therefore seems appropriate for me to concentrate on the main lines only. In order not to have to deal with all the outdated attempts to solve problems, I will merely quote, in the following summary, L. Goppelt's assessment of the so-called purely historical method, which roughly dates to the nineteenth century and belongs to the exegetical phraseology that extends to the First World War (and certainly also after this). He reasons,

> "Purely historical" did not mean objective scientific method. As E. Troeltsch himself clarified, "an entire world view" was operative as rational presupposition. Had it not been the intention here to emancipate biblical research through the historical-critical principle in order to make such research all the more independent of the philosophies of particular epochs? Was not this the goal of wresting such from the domain of ecclesiastical tradition, from the categories—as was often said—of metaphysics? Was there to be a solution to this dilemma? Was one not unavoidably bound to the rational presuppositions of one's time?[1]

Space does not permit close investigation of such movements as the Tübingen School, the (original) religious historical school, or (classical) liberal theology, and so we move directly on to the hermeneutical reorientation, which started to take shape shortly after World War I. Two names play particular and major roles here: those of Karl Barth and Rudolf Bultmann.[2]

Personally, I would add yet another name: Dietrich Bonhoeffer. It is odd that he has not gained more public attention in the discussion concerning the principles of the philosophical prerequisites of theology. Yet his *Habilitationsschrift, Akt und Sein* (1931)[3] truly deserves consideration in this context. Incidentally, Barth and Bultmann have already been submitted to careful study and multiple critical reappraisals. There is not much left to be studied in regard to their hermeneutical input—except, perhaps, for someone whose field is the history of dogma—whereas to date, Bonhoeffer's contribution has not been sufficiently scrutinized. The time is finally ripe for him to break through the prison walls and into academic freedom (albeit with all its prejudice against those who think differently).

An Interesting Debate at the Turn of the Twentieth Century

Before going into the actual theme, I wish to give a brief account of an interesting debate from the turn of the twentieth century. It dealt with the suitability of various methods in the discipline of theology and touched upon the issue of hermeneutics. Thus it is appropriate to refer to the older discussion here. Incidentally, my impression is that around the turn of the twentieth century, scholars were at least a bit more aware of the general philosophical prerequisites of academia as a result of the new orientation brought about by the collapse of neo-Protestantism. The methodological consideration was characterized at that time by a thoroughness and versatility one seldom encounters today.[4] In this day and age, theologians are often lulled into accepting given premises and ready concepts without ever realizing the need to reflect more closely on these, let alone to question them. Even a cursory review of the past deepens the understanding of the hermeneutical prerequisites characteristic of modern theology. Following the survey, a critical analysis dealing with the hermeneutics of Barth, Bultmann, and Bonhoeffer will be provided in the next chapter.

The abovementioned debate was launched by P. Jäger's provocative article *Das "atheistische Denken" der neueren Theologie*.[5] He energetically defends "atheistic methods" as the only scientific set of tools for theological research. His bold opinion caused an immediate reaction. A. Schlatter wrote a very comprehensive response, *Atheistische Methoden in der Theologie*, where he vigorously defended the unique status of the theological discipline against Jäger.[6] In the following discussion, I will let both parties have their say without much interference in their debate. I will present my own opinion later.

Above all, the debate between Jäger and Schlatter deals with the issue of what *academic discipline*[7] is all about. Jäger writes,

> [Academic discipline means] that in their work, the entire scientific community leaves the idea of God out of the picture and with rigid consistency strives to explain the world on the basis of the world itself. One should, after all, be so fair as to admit that as the matter stands, academic discipline indeed *can* have no other methods.[8]

Schlatter responds,

> His [viz. Jäger's] concept of the world, which posits an enclosed system of viewing the entire realm of what takes place in the world so that nothing is allowed to come into consideration apart from the world itself, is itself a system of dogmatics; however it is a dogmatics without values, if for no other reason than that it is not worked out and substantiated.[9]

Then Jäger and Schlatter debate the position of theology at the university. Jäger writes,

> For theology can only have legitimate status within the *Universitas Litterarum* as long as it sincerely and honestly, and not only in

pretense, employs generally accepted scientific methods. If theology cannot, then it must have the resolve to leave the field.[10]

Schlatter's response is as follows:

> The atheistic approach to theology would in any case be the most certain means of destroying the theological faculties. Once our students read the New Testament in the same manner that they read Homer, and our exegetes interpret it as they do with Homer with a determined exclusion of every thought oriented towards God, then it is over for the theological faculties.[11]

Next, Jäger and Schlatter discuss the relationship between piety and academic discipline. Jäger writes,

> When we distinguish academic discipline and piety as two separate forms of making the same content relevant for today, it can no longer be considered outrageous when theologians also use the religiously indifferent "historical" and "immanent" methods in their field.[12]

Schlatter responds,

> Now, however, when theology has also become atheistic, what is the source of "higher knowledge"? If the theologian certainly does not speak the last, most profound word, who then speaks it? In any case, not the New Testament, as we have indeed "interpreted it without the utilization of the idea of God."[13]

Finally, one more quotation by Schlatter, where he very subtly shapes the difficult problems of academic theology, will be helpful:

> Now, however, when we wish to explain religion from the standpoint of the world, we place ourselves, from the outset and logically, in a radical contradiction to the object of our study, which simply does not wish to be explained from the standpoint of the world, but rather loudly and persistently asserts the idea of God. The object of our study intends that we think about God; the observer thinks "without

taking the idea of God into consideration." [. . .] And the more we
want to explain rather than merely observe, the more our object will
be forced into our ready-made model, the stronger the scientific car-
icature will become, and the more certain the alleged academic discipline is transformed into polemics against the object that we are
studying. In this way, we do not portray what is real but rather a novel
presented by the historian.[14]

Theological Research in the Shadow of Kant

Jäger's argumentation in the abovementioned debate gives witness
to the clear but often latent influence that Immanuel Kant and his
line of thought have had and still have on the academic world and
especially the theological discipline. He successfully combined
seventeenth-century rationalism (René Descartes, Baruch Spinoza,
and Gottfried Leibniz) with eighteenth-century empiricism (John
Locke, George Berkeley, and David Hume) into a fascinating new
scheme. According to the first approach, the foundation for knowledge is reason (consciousness), but according to the latter, it is
sense perception (experience).[15] Kant insisted that both are partly
right (or partly wrong). He argued that knowledge about the world
comes through the senses but is organized and processed with
the help of reason, which ultimately determines how each person
interprets the world. It is not possible, then, to know with certainty
the "thing in itself" (*das Ding an sich*, or *noumena*), only the "thing
for myself" (*das Ding für mich*, or *phenomena*). Science is occupied
with things as they reveal themselves to human reason through
experience. Hence no one should postulate that God inevitably
exists. In any case, his alleged involvement in the course of history
is outside of causation and intellectual comprehension. There is,
however, a void within the sphere of ethics and aesthetics where
belief in Deity finds its proper role. You can meet your God at that
place, though only in a highly subjective—never objective—way.
In other words, his furthest "outpost" lies at the periphery of the
philosophical system.[16]

Accordingly, an atheistic principle characterizes Kant's thinking.[17] His philosophy dismantles traditional metaphysics and biblical
theology. They are reduced to issues belonging to the realm of strong

subjective interest without any objective reality. On the whole, the Kantian shift in philosophy launched an influential Copernican revolution in human disciplines that still permeates modern hermeneutics to a great extent.[18] It turns the succeeding philosophical developments into variations on the fundamental dualism between scientific objectivity in the sphere of nature and history and subjectivity in the sphere of religious experience (as will be briefly shown below).[19]

The Long Arm of Kantianism

To a large degree, several of the new exegetical methods find their roots in Kant's philosophical system. The skepticism he has, at least in a strictly academic setting, for metaphysics—that is, God's existence and involvement in the course of history—is now applied to the text itself. The author gets to represent "the God of the text." What he wants to express remains ultimately unclear because he does not "possess" his own text. On the contrary, it has arisen as a result of different political, economic, cultural, religious, and ethical factors and is reinterpreted each time it is read from readers' related (but more or less distinctive) circumstances. Therefore, the meaning is constantly changing and is never actually fixed to a particular content or a single purpose. In the deepest sense, the exegete decides what the text stands for. Without his interpretation, the text becomes silent and cannot be heard. Exegesis is transformed (or distorted) to eisegesis. In reality, the principle of "anything goes" reigns supreme. Consequently, the question of the difference between the biblical text and its commentary arises: Is there any at all?[20]

From this postmodern way of doing research, two main paths have emerged. The first, called pragmatism, develops primarily from Charles Sanders Peirce's philosophy and emphasizes using the text as it is without even looking for the original meaning. The second, called deconstructionism, initially derives from Ferdinand de Saussure (even if Jacques Derrida probably is more well known for popularizing the idea) and emphasizes analyzing the text to find out the different (often) hidden intentions behind the external meaning. As a result of these two main paths, Kant's philosophical proposition has

been run in absurdum specifically in the realm of interpretive real-
ism. Or maybe the limitations in his criticism of metaphysics have
been exposed that way.[21]

Postmodern trends in their most radical form hardly ever take
root in biblical scholarship.[22] Nevertheless, Kantianism is, no doubt,
the philosophical hotbed of contemporary methodological neoori-
entations. At least part of the hermeneutical problem in current
research is already present here.

A Postmodern Kantianism—a Stranded Ism

On the whole, the postmodern relativism of interpretation running
in absurdum with constantly changing meanings raises a question
concerning the rationale of all academic discussion: If no one can
express original thoughts and views to others without being reinterpreted or misinterpreted by them, what is left of communication
and discourse? In that case, there is no room for scholarly discussion and interaction. The proponents of deconstructionism jettison
and dump the conventional characteristics of the human exchange
of ideas. They deconstruct and devastate even their own speculative theories, ultimately asserting that whatever they write is not
to be understood by their readers. Only total desolation remains in
absolute isolation.

The radical skepticism of deconstructionism about the effec-
tiveness of the language to convey an authentic message from the
speaker (author) to the hearer (reader) never makes headway among
the common people and hardly gains broad agreement among scholars. Furthermore, those few who do consent to the theory of max-
imum doubt are, according to the very same theory, ultimately not
able to mediate their cynicism to the others! Still, with their nota-
ble contribution, they have shed more light on the methodological
basics of academic research. They have brought Kantianism to an
extreme where there is no exit or escape from a chaos of meaning.

A Way Out of Kantianism

The incessant fluctuation of comprehension and interpretation, embedded in deconstructionism, ceases only if there is a factual correlation between language and reality corresponding to an everyday experience. Then it ought to be expected that what I am saying (writing) is what you are hearing (reading). Obvious misunderstandings might be cleared up. In general, this kind of ordinary common sense is assumed. Yet where does it come from? There is one simple answer: it is based on nothing else but God's solid creation. He invented the human language, which correlates with reality. Here indeed ends the constant change of meaning presumed within deconstructionism. The cosmos has a well-defined structure that is to be organized and articulated through language. Any other conclusion takes the academic discussion down a blind alley and leads to a kind of self-imposed blockade.[23]

Startlingly, that's why every human being presupposes God's existence in his everyday experience and even in his more speculative reflections. There is finally no escape from that fact notwithstanding that someone in his thinking imagines an atheistic or an agnostic point of departure. Indeed, only a "fool says in his heart, 'There is no God'" (Ps. 14:1, 53:1). How true! Hence atheism and agnosticism have already been stranded or shipwrecked before being launched or set afloat. The so-called God hypothesis is to be denied neither in our ordinary discussions nor in our complicated academic conversations. Whoever you are, you are and you remain *Homo religiosus*. Not perceiving and admitting this, then you become *Homo idioticus*.

Therefore, it does not make any sense to take for granted that Christian scholars have to play with atheistic or agnostic "rules of the game," doing their high-level research in the academic world. To be sure, the general revelation of God's existence stands out as the starting point of all scientific studies at the university. There is a true reality out there, outside us and beyond our human minds. It is based on creation and mastered especially through verbal communication in academic contexts. Believe it or not, the "God hypothesis" is the well-founded axiom for any proper knowledge.[24]

Moreover, with regard to the Kantian (or post-Enlightenment) assumptions concerning the individual as autonomous and self-determining, it is questionable whether such an individual existed in the first-century Hellenistic world.[25] All Cartesian oppositions (matter versus nonmatter, nature versus supranature, physicality versus spirituality, corporeality versus psychology) are totally misleading when retroactively projected into ancient language.[26] Indeed, there is no abstract concept of the person. The modern individualist self, rooted in an idealistic philosophy, is an illusion. Individuality presupposes relationality. It is said that "no man is an island"[27] and "you have to be addressed as a subject to become one."[28] The person primarily exists, not in self-relation, but rather in relational exchange. He or she is embodied and embedded in his or her world. In the theology of the Bible, a close interplay prevails between social human relations and suprahuman realities that affect the cosmos. To excise those elements from the overall picture would result in a shadowy or gloomy image.[29]

Conditio Sine Qua Non for the Theological Discipline

The latest development within biblical scholarship has brought about some positive outcomes. With the entrance of postmodern approaches, historical criticism's position as the dominant method has begun to unravel. Saying this does not seem unscientific any longer.[30] It is now recognized, more widely than ever, that the same texts are to be interpreted from many different perspectives. Yet the criticism of the historical-critical approach occasionally goes too far. By and large, the method does not fall short due to the principal request for meaning or simple facts encompassed in the sources. Rather, the basic atheistic presuppositions comprised in it have a disastrous effect (as will be argued below).[31]

The previous somewhat heated discussion between Jäger and Schlatter reveals a difficulty in combining theological research with academic precepts as they have come to be accepted (by whom, no one seems to know, however). Correspondingly, endless discussions would just as well take place within our intellectual environments. To reconcile the dispute probably borders on the irrational, as the debate has been at a standstill so long. Apparently, both parties have held their place mutatis mutandis. Now I would like to draw attention to new avenues of study. The current understanding of the legitimate premises of academia needs to be modified, or rather, the unique status of theological research should be demonstrated.

A theologian's task, so clear, is to talk about God—that is, to proclaim God's word. Theology, the word being from the Greek *theos* ("God") and *logos* ("word"), as a scholarly discipline deals *per definitionem* with a doctrine of God. Scholarship that starts with the concept that there is no God (or at least there is no God that one can include) cannot, in the deepest sense of the meaning, perform *theological* research. In that case, perhaps it seems necessary to simply remove theological research from its connection with the university and establish ecclesiastical institutes with particular theological orientations instead. As a result, we would at least recognize that present-day academic theology is incapable of studying all that interests us as human beings. This conclusion goes against the general understanding of the function of academia. Why should academics leave (*real*) theological issues outside the realm of theological discipline? On the other hand, it certainly appears difficult to accept a working hypothesis of "God" in the exegetical study of biblical texts. In a nutshell, this is where our main problem lies.[32]

If we are involved in *true* theological research, God's existence and his intervention in history cannot and must not be excluded. A theologian whose comprehensive work is based on atheistic methods is stranded in a sheer conflict: he is engaged in biblical texts that tell about God's agency in the course of history, and nevertheless he utilizes methods that do not even allow God to exist.[33] A person measuring two liters of milk with a tape measure or weighing ten kilograms of potatoes with a ruler would be just as successful.[34] In the final analysis, we must ask ourselves whether it is legitimate to define the concept "academic theology" in an atheistic manner—that is, without allowing for a "supernatural reality." Academic disciplines always hold to a variety of self-evident premises or axioms that are to a certain extent dependent on the field of research at hand. Consequently, it is by no means arbitrary to draw the conclusion, at least for academic theology, that a factual openness toward God's sovereign intervention in history must principally prevail. Otherwise, we have no theology in any real sense of the word.[35]

An Academic Assessment of the So-Called Historical-Critical Method

As will have become apparent, from a specifically *academic* perspective, we have to take a reserved stance on the so-called historical critical method within the discipline of theology. A method that does not at all do justice to the distinctive characteristics of the sources and their main intents can hardly be recommended. It is, however, not different methodological tools or minor features that primarily lead to the fatal distortion of research but rather the underlying hermeneutics in its totality. The historical-critical method is primarily based on two (very frequently unmentioned) premises.

(1) Understanding of History

God cannot affect the course of history. Neither is it certain that he even exists. In the best case, he resides somewhere far out in heaven—where he will remain forever. History is totally human. Without any conceit, God cannot be compared to an extraterrestrial alien who is claimed to pay an occasional visit to the earth. He only has the right to live in the religious thoughts of a scholar.

(2) Critical Stance

We human beings are the ones who take a critical stance toward Holy Scripture. It is true that a scholar must always work critically (cf., e.g., textual or source criticism),[36] but in this case, his methodological approach coincides with a deceitful prejudice against the Bible's foremost message, which deals with the revelation of God's intervention in the miserable mess of the world. In the spirit of such criticism and in the name of scholarly research, even the first-class exegetes reach results that inevitably remain a distortion. With their limited point of departure, they initially lack a sense of what is most essential.[37]

Hence the former considerations are not directed against the meaning of grammatical, linguistic, semantic, or rhetorical analyses; form-critical observations; textual-, source-, or redaction-critical accounts; and so forth even though I indeed do not wish to subscribe to *all* the results attained. Especially within Old Testament exegetics, in my opinion—without going further into the problematic issues—features such as overemphasized redaction critical aspects prevail.[38] But still *abusus non tollit usum*. We are allowed and able to use a whole set of methodological tools in order to understand biblical texts, provided that we start with another hermeneutical perspective or engage other hermeneutical principles than those that have been established until now (see below).[39]

The Crisis of Protestantism

In using the historical-critical method, Protestant churches have to a great extent lost sight of the Bible as God's word. It is all about God's word without God! Consequently, human traditions rule again. They again gain a clear upper hand over the Bible. This time around, however, the focus lies on the professors' specific monographs and the bishops' latest proclamations. For certain, they carry the most weight.[40] Perhaps the Lutheran world has suffered the worst from such a development. Even many conservative circles within various Protestant denominations seem to have no other option than to emphasize the authority of the Bible in the church as a *norma normans*, though they do not hold to its divine origin within the realm of academia. So they lack a clear identity. Their shortage paralyzes their work for spiritual renewal and further results in a suppressed conflict within the sphere of academia. Anyone who excludes God in accordance with the dictum of academia and then seeks to create faith in him on account of the message of the church is stranded in a religious schizophrenia, unable to convince the modern listener of that much.[41]

In order to overcome the problematic state of affairs to which the unique status of the theological discipline gives rise, principally K. Barth and R. Bultmann, as stated, set out to look for a fresh holistic solution in the range of hermeneutics. The former represents the Reformed groups within Protestantism, while the latter is rather closer to the Lutheran persuasion. I will direct my attention toward their positions in the following section.

Biblical Hermeneutics

A Christological Perspective

The Hermeneutical Dilemma of K. Barth and R. Bultmann

Within the bounds of a short survey, it is not possible to draw on an exhaustive study of the comprehensive scholarly work of Barth and Bultmann, so I will be content to point out certain characteristic features in their hermeneutics that touch upon my own theme.

Barth represents what we call *dialectic theology*. He places emphasis on divine revelation. God is transcendent and sovereign. We human beings have no interaction with him, not even so much as a point of contact with his supernatural world. An impenetrable wall exists between Creator and creation. Both parties live in total isolation from each other. Human beings have no way of getting in contact with God. He appears to them "senkrecht von oben" (straight from above).[1] Yet revelation does not coincide with the Bible, as the Bible only bears witness to revelation.[2] Thus even the reading of the Holy Scriptures does not guarantee that we human beings find a remedy for our loneliness. We remain in our misery. Thus Barth's position is rightly called *atheistic anthropology*.[3]

Bultmann, on the other hand, represents the so-called *existential theology*. He intensively seeks to rescue the early church's original kerygma from behind the mythological use of language in the New Testament, which seems to be incomprehensible to the modern and secularized person. Demythologization means that the "true apostolic message," directed at a new understanding of ourselves and of all existence, emerges clearly and distinctly. In this context, however, concrete events within the *Heilsgeschichte* (the history of salvation)—such as the virgin birth and resurrection, as well as miracles—no longer play any role. They can be interpreted as secondary material only serving as links to a greater "inner truth."[4] On account of this, I would call Bultmann's position *atheistic soteriology*.

So it is perhaps a bit surprising that atheistic undertones have characterized the theological reorientation ever since World War I. We must actually ask ourselves whether Barth and Bultmann truly managed to free themselves from the hermeneutical legacy of the nineteenth century, mainly composed of (even if hidden) atheism.[5] With Barth's atheistic anthropology and Bultmann's atheistic soteriology, we run into the same problems that have been explained above. A theologian must not accept any atheistic point of view as his hermeneutical starting point. He should dare to be a theologian! Under such circumstances it does not seem altogether strange that hardly anything tangible remained from the theological reorientation after World War I.

Besides Barth and Bultmann, Dietrich Bonhoeffer also strove to overcome the hermeneutical dilemma, attempting not to allow an atheistic premise to determine the final result. His theses have not been submitted to careful scrutiny thus far. So it is appropriate to discuss his approach in more depth.[6]

D. Bonhoeffer's Attempt to Solve the Hermeneutic Dilemma

Bonhoeffer works toward the sort of theological perspective that gives justice to the unique statuses of the sources without preconceived reservations. According to him, divine revelation is of a contingent nature—that is, it does not adapt to the limitations or demands of reason.[7] Deep down, we human beings can never understand ourselves by ourselves. We are incapable of placing our own existence in light of the truth. It is only divine revelation that can do this. Conversion takes place by God's mercy, which is at work in the congregation.[8] Thus human existence is found either "in Adam" or "in Christ." The transfer from Adam to Christ depends on a miracle: the one who knows the truth is already known by the Truth.[9] In that manner Bonhoeffer manages to define the relationship between *Akt* (*die reine Intentionalität, gerichtet auf*; i.e., "faith") and *Sein* (i.e., "revelation") in a satisfactory manner.[10] To quote him at some length:

> Faith is "in reference to" being (community of faith); it is only in faith that being discloses itself, or "is" (community of faith). But faith knows this being as independent of itself, while knowing itself to be one of the manners of being of being itself. Being transcends something that exists; it is the ground of being of that which exists, as of the I. Thus, act comes from being, just as it proceeds towards being. On its part, being is in reference to act and yet free. The being-of-revelation is "person," hovering in the tension between the objective and nonobjective, the revealed person of God and the personal community that is founded on God's person. Here the transcendental approach of "being only in the act" unexpectedly coalesces with the original ontological principle of the freedom of being vis-à-vis the act, of the suspension of the act in being.[11]

Therefore, the fact that Bonhoeffer interprets the congregation as being in a personal relationship with Christ is a necessary prerequisite for his understanding of revelation. God reveals himself in Christ, who commits himself to the congregation. Hence it is not possible to control his revelation through human reason (no matter how sharp and sound someone's thinking may be).

Through his dynamic understanding of revelation, Bonhoeffer gets rid of the direct counterarguments that earlier research (including that performed by Barth and Bultmann) had been guilty of as we have already seen. Instead of any philosophical speculation, he wants to direct his attention to the actual content of "real" or "true" theology—that is, to the living Christ.[12]

A short extract from Bonhoeffer's position cannot satisfactorily reveal his extremely strong argumentation and vivid style. It is a theological masterpiece with many thought-provoking passages rich in aphorisms; it is a book definitely well worth reading. But for now this summary must suffice. In the following discussion, I will try to take the debate further and elucidate an aspect of the matter that I believe Bonhoeffer did not take into full consideration and that yet deserves careful scrutiny. In the final analysis, it is Bonhoeffer's own theses that will thereby be confirmed.

The Completion of Bonhoeffer's Hermeneutics

De facto Bonhoeffer does not explain what revelation actually is. He does not seem to identify it directly with the Bible. To be sure, Bonhoeffer does repeatedly talk about the word, proclamation, and sermon as basic elements of the congregation. His argumentation is certainly tied to the thought that the Old and New Testaments are canonical books. Still, he criticizes Lutheran orthodoxy for its identification of revelation with the Bible.[13] How, then, do revelation and the Bible relate to each other? Bonhoeffer never gives an answer in his book. He is content to argue for a sociological (i.e., ecclesiological) aspect of revelation. He does this for a good reason. Nevertheless, the reader easily gains the impression that something essential is missing. A sociological aspect seems to be a fairly narrow point of view. Could it be that Bonhoeffer has drawn isolated conclusions about revelation in his *Habilitationsschrift*, *Akt und Sein* from his dissertation *Sanctorum communio* without actually broadening his ecclesiological perspective to a noticeable extent?[14] This is a fascinating thought.

It is impossible for me to go into the relationship of Lutheran orthodoxy with the Bible here. Yet it is my opinion that rumor, in this case, is worse than reality. To take an example, Hermann Sasse, another famous systematician in Germany, was later forced to change his rather negative criticism in the face of indisputable facts.[15] In the following discussion, I would like to draw attention only to the solidification of the content of revelation, a theme that Bonhoeffer, as stated, does not adequately take into consideration.

If revelation is attached to the presence of Christ in the congregation through the word, at least two questions remain:

1. What is the relationship of revelation to the word of the Bible? Bonhoeffer rightly points out that genuine revelation cannot be subjected to any human system or

control. According to him, it must retain its freedom, its
contingency.[16]

2. What is the relationship of revelation to the central message of the Bible, justification by faith? Here again genuine
   revelation cannot be reduced to a *system*-based orthodoxy, which allows itself to be subjected to the authority
   of various theologians.[17]

A Bonhoefferian answer to the questions posed above would
strive to follow his type of argumentation in favor of the ecclesiological aspect of revelation: in order to retain the contingent and dynamic
nature of revelation, it sounds plausible also to personify the Bible
and its central message—in other words, to understand all this in a
personal relation to Christ. Incidentally, in the context of his work,
Bonhoeffer criticizes both the institution of the Roman Catholic
Church and the view of the Bible held by Lutheran orthodoxy. He
justifies the former critique through reference to the personified
character of the congregation—that is, its personal relation to Christ.
Strangely enough, however, he does not in the slightest justify his
latter criticism.[18] If a reader were to continue with Bonhoeffer's vein
of thought, it would follow logically that he also in that case would
come to emphasize the personified character of the Bible—that is, its
personal relation to Christ (something that should not be strange to
theologians in Lutheran orthodoxy). The same argumentation prevails, then, with the application of the central message of the Bible,
justification by faith.

Thus we face the traditional phrase "Christ the core and star"
(*Kern und Stern*) of the Scriptures. But what does such an expression
actually entail? D. A. Carson rightly cautions against generalizations
in this context: "How does one avoid generalities? One might say
that the center of NT theology is Jesus Christ, but although at one
level that is saying everything at another level it is saying almost
nothing."[19]

In this matter, Bonhoeffer falls short. He does not solidify the
content of revelation sufficiently but primarily struggles with only
the general prerequisites of revelation. Naturally, it seems credible,
against the background of the overwhelming coverage of the Bible,

to blame almost anyone for insufficient solidification, but on account of the above reasons, I believe we have established grounds for the need to complete Bonhoeffer's argument. Accordingly, I intend to submit the Epistle to the Romans, the apostle Paul's main work, to closer scrutiny according to the definition of my assignment. If necessary, I will also certainly consult the other Pauline Epistles.

The Anthropology of Paul's Hermeneutics

Before going further, it is still worth emphasizing one thing. The anthropology Bonhoeffer presupposes in his hermeneutics, assuming the total inability of human beings by their own power to come to terms with the revelation (see above), no doubt corresponds to the theological intent of Romans. Conclusive evidence has been substantiated and documented already in another context.[20]

Thus the Kantian or post-Enlightenment assumption about the individual as an autonomous and self-determining subject is overturned.[21] There is no freestanding self who is able to remain impartial and evaluate, let alone choose, between different possible identities. Nor is there a neutral environment within which we may act out our personal lives as we like.[22] The whole of humankind is involved in the realm of sin and death. Everyone is guilty for his or her part as he or she offends the divine will. And yet no one escapes the tyranny of the demonic powers under which all the transgressions come to pass. As evidence, "the sin" (ἡ ἁμαρτία) exerts a transsubjective reign of terror over the cosmos in Rom. 5–7: "Sin came into the world through the fall of Adam (5:12) and gained dominion (5:21). Man is enslaved to it (6:6, 6:17–23) or stands under its authority (6:13). Sin renders the salary of death to the sinner (6:23). It takes occasion by the law to excite lust in man, to deceive and to kill him (7:8, 7:11, 7:13). The 'I' is sold under sin (7:14). It dwells and acts in him (7:17, 20)."[23]

Similarly, "the flesh" (ἡ σάρξ) has attained transsubjective supremacy: "The flesh has its own works (Gal. 5:19) and actions (Rom. 8:13), passions and lusts (Gal. 5:24). In addition, it has a mind hostilely directed against God, one which does not submit to the law of God (Rom. 8:6–7). The flesh lusts against the Spirit and hinders the believer from doing good (Gal. 5:17). The Christian runs the danger of becoming anew a 'debtor' of the flesh (Rom. 8:12) or opening the gate to the flesh (Gal. 5:13)."[24]

On the other hand, salvation brings about a new relational union characterized by undeserved and noncompetitive grace. It suggests human involvement in an interpersonal regime inaugurated and indwelt by Christ.[25]

The Hermeneutics of Romans

To begin with, the theme (propositio) of Romans admonishes the reader to pay attention to its most important content. This is presented in Rom. 1:16–17: "I am not ashamed of the gospel, for it is the power of God for salvation to everyone who believes, to the Jew first and also to the Greek. For in it the righteousness of God is revealed from faith for faith, as it is written, 'The righteous shall live by faith.'"[26]

I will paraphrase the verses in the following manner: the gospel as God's power reveals righteousness from Him for salvation to all (meaning Jews and Gentiles) who believe in Christ in accordance with the Old Testament.

Hence the Epistle to the Romans wants to testify to at least three main theses: the gospel as God's power

1. reveals justification by faith,
2. is in harmony with the Old Testament, and
3. concerns all, both Jews and Gentiles.[27]

In fact, these three main theses take on the same issues that the above discussion with Bonhoeffer entailed. The first point focuses on the central scriptural message, the second on the significance of the Holy Scriptures, and the third on the unity of the congregation. In this way, scrutiny of the Epistle to the Romans matches amazingly well with the hermeneutical considerations given in the previous sections. In addition, the three main theses cover the general content in Romans. The first point corresponds to the explanation of righteousness through faith in 1:18–8:39, the second to the stance on Israel and its holy tradition in chapters 9–11, and the third to the encouragement of mutual love in chapters 12–15.[28] In the following, I will deal with the different parts in reverse order.

(1) The Congregation—the Body of Christ

The situation in Rome was marked by a considerably broad division among the Christians. Apparently, they had gathered from the very start in various synagogues of the capital city. Their breaking away from the Jewish religion then brought about the birth of several separate congregations. Actually, there was no such thing as a united congregation. Paul does not address his epistle to a *single* congregation in Rome. Quite the contrary, he directs a great number of his general salutations in chapter 16 to separate house churches.[29] In the way of the creation of one single congregation stood controversies over permitted foods and conflicts over festivals, which made it difficult to celebrate communion together in the worship service (containing the real mealtime). Some opponents represented "the weak" in faith and refrained especially from food offered to idols, while others, "the strong" in faith, ate everything.[30]

Paul intervenes in the conflict as early as chapter 12 but in greater detail as late as chapter 14. From among his thorough argumentation, I will take up only one point, which plays an important role in this context: The unity of the congregation has its foundation first and foremost in Christ. Believers form one single body in him: "For as in one body we have many members, and the members do not all have the same function, so we, though many, are one body in Christ, and individually members one of another" (Rom. 12:4–5). From this comes not only the insight about the many facets of gifts (12:6–8) but also an exhortation to patience and mutual love (chapter 14). The same thought pattern emerges, incidentally, in 1 Cor. 12–13. There the apostle explains first the unity of the congregation as the body of Christ (12:12–26), then underlines the multifaceted nature of the gifts (12:27–30a; see already vv. 4–11), and finally affirms the supremacy of love (12:31b–13:7; cf. vv. 8–13). Even though Paul shares the view of the strong in the purity of all foods, he does not wish to force the weak to accept something that goes against their conscience, while on the other hand he does not want the weak to judge the strong either. Both parties are to live in sincere love and mutual respect (12:9–10)—namely, in accordance with the spiritual fellowship that already prevails between them through Christ and that is to be preserved as much as possible.[31]

In light of Paul's reasoning in the Epistle to the Romans, Bonhoeffer's presentation on the unity of the congregation in Christ thus does not lack support. His hermeneutical premise for the theological interpretation of revelation has thereby been confirmed.

(2) The Holy Scriptures—Christ's Testimony of Himself

Right at the beginning of the Epistle to the Romans, Paul defines his stance on the Old Testament texts. His gospel promotes Christ as one "he [God] promised beforehand through his prophets in the holy Scriptures" (1:2). Here presumably *all* the authors of the Old Testament are counted as prophets. They have spoken of the Son of God's incarnation, death, and resurrection (vv. 3–4). The Scriptures are called "holy" since they are by nature totally different from all the other texts. So Paul does not read the Old Testament as just any other book. There he finds a prophetic route to the New Testament, the foundation for his kerygma, something to which he will later bear witness as well.[32]

At the end of the Epistle to the Romans, Paul again sharpens his view on the Old Testament texts. There he praises God, who is "able to strengthen you according to [his] gospel and the preaching of Jesus Christ [or perhaps 'Jesus' proclamation'], according to the revelation of the mystery that was kept secret for long ages but has now been disclosed and through the prophetic writings has been made known to all nations, according to the command of the eternal God, to bring about the obedience of faith" (16:25–26).[33]

The final doxology appears almost incomprehensible: the gospel reveals the secret that was hidden but is already there in the *Old* Testament! What does Paul mean with such a seemingly contradictory expression? He thinks that the new revelation in and through Christ broadens the perspective and brings out a viewpoint that allows the message of the Scriptures to come out as a three-dimensional picture. Hence it is the gospel that opens the locked secrets in the Old Testament. We must therefore not read the Old Testament "between the lines" or "from behind the text" but literally and at the same time in faith with regard to the factual content—namely, Christ.[34]

So at both the beginning and the end of the Epistle to the Romans, Paul emphasizes that he has wanted to cast light on the Old Testament. This coincides with statistical facts: over half of all the Old Testament quotations in the Pauline Epistles appear in the Epistle to the Romans.[35]

Luther also comes to the same conclusion in his preface to the Epistle to the Romans:

> In this epistle we thus find most abundantly the things that a Christian ought to know, namely, what is law, gospel, sin, punishment, grace, faith, righteousness, Christ, God, good works, love, hope, and the cross; and also how we are to conduct ourselves toward everyone, be he righteous or sinner, strong or weak, friend or foe—and even toward our own selves. Moreover this is all ably supported with Scripture and proved by St. Paul's own example and that of the prophets, so that one could not wish for anything more. Therefore it appears that he wanted in this one epistle to sum up briefly the whole Christian and evangelical doctrine, and to prepare an introduction to the entire Old Testament. For, without doubt, whoever has this epistle well in his heart, has with him the light and power of the Old Testament. Therefore let every Christian be familiar with it and exercise himself in it continually. To this end may God give his grace. Amen.[36]

In light of the above rather concise survey of the Epistle to the Romans, the apostle Paul explains the Old Testament texts in a clearly Christocentric manner, with their "personal relation" to Christ (the same train of thought appears, e.g., in 2 Cor. 3:14–18). From his method of argumentation, it follows that the completion of Bonhoeffer's hermeneutical input is in this respect based on sufficient evidence. In the following chapter, I will further delineate Paul's understanding of the Scriptures.

(3) God's Righteousness—Christ Himself

According to the theme of the Epistle to the Romans per the above discussion, Paul confirms that "God's righteousness" appears in the gospel (1:17). In his presentation of himself, he offers as his apostolic assignment (1:1) to proclaim the gospel about God's Son (1:3), or Jesus Christ the Lord (1:4). "God's righteousness" and "God's Son, Jesus Christ" are juxtaposed with one another. In essence, they have the same meaning. Incidentally, M. Seifrid comes to the same conclusion, although via another route of study. He argues in the following manner:

> It is "in the gospel" that "the righteousness of God" is revealed. Paul's localizing declaration suggests that he refers to the resurrection of the crucified Christ, employing biblical language in order to convey its saving significance. "God's righteousness" is his "vindicating act" of raising Christ from the dead for us.[37]

Later on Seifrid presents a similar interpretation concerning Rom. 10:4. He claims, "Later in Romans, Paul identifies Christ with the revealed 'righteousness of God' to which Israel refused to submit."[38]

In addition, such an interpretation is strengthened by the close relationship between 9:30–33 and 10:1–3. The arguments in both passages correspond to each other in the following ways:

- pursuing a law of righteousness (9:31)—being zealous for God (10:2)
- "as if it were based on works" (9:32)—establishing one's own righteousness (10:3)
- to stumble over the stumbling stone (9:32), that is, Christ (9:33)—not to submit to God's righteousness (10:3), that is, Christ (10:4), who by himself has brought about the righteousness (10:5–8)[39]

Since Christ himself represents "God's righteousness," it is really not at all strange that "righteousness by faith" *speaks* (as if it were a living person) in v. 6–8 (cf. similar language in Gal. 3:23–25).[40]

The perspective at least implied in the Epistle to the Romans appears then loud and clear in the two Epistles to the Corinthians. The righteousness of the Christians coincides there with Christ. The most relevant places are 1 Cor. 1:30 and 2 Cor. 5:21. According to the former verse, the believers exist "in Christ Jesus, who became to us [. . .] from God, righteousness." According to the latter verse, reconciliation means that "in him (viz. Christ) we might become the righteousness of God."[41] Apart from this, Paul says about himself that he seeks righteousness in Christ (Gal. 2:17) and that he hopes to be found in Christ with "righteousness from God" (Phil. 3:9).[42]

The abovementioned biblical passages prove without a doubt that righteousness is understood as a personal relationship to Christ and even as being identified with him. Therefore, in this respect, too, the completion of Bonhoeffer's hermeneutics is based on sufficient evidence.

Evaluation of the Results

The atheistic undertone that in the deepest sense characterizes academic theology as a whole inevitably leads to a dead end. The hermeneutics of Romans (and Bonhoeffer's analysis of the comprehensive nature of revelation) shows the way forward. Here, Christ is at the center: he constitutes and is the congregation, he exists in Scripture, and he represents God's righteousness in his own person. The rather short study of the Epistle to the Romans has thus defined content in contingent revelation more closely. Also, the broadening of the perspective involved serves to protect contingent revelation against a more or less arbitrary interpretation. For if revelation simply "happens" in the congregation, the objective criteria for judging a genuine versus false revelation are missing. Long ago, Scholastic theology became stranded in a serious crisis on the basis of a diffuse definition of the intrinsic criteria of revelation. Its concurrent system included pure arbitrariness that progressively promoted the Catholic clergy's hegemony and authority over the Bible.[43]

In the above discussion, however, I still have not explained the matter completely. There are at least two remaining issues. First, we must sharpen the Christocentric interpretation of the Bible in order to arrange the material for presentation. Second, we need to think further about the relationship between *Akt* and *Sein*, starting with the completion of Bonhoeffer's stance. The question that deserves special attention is whether revelation, solidly anchored in the Bible and its central message, again forms a static system that human beings can control with their reason. Then we would have lost the contingent nature of revelation while hoping to define its special content more closely. For the above reasons, I intend to continue my study of the Epistle to the Romans. I am searching for a dynamic view of the Bible.

IV

Paul's Way of Reading Holy Scripture

Main Thesis

The authority of Scripture is the very foundation upon which the argumentation of Romans begins. Immediately after Paul introduces himself to the church in Rome as the apostle to the Gentiles (1:1), he talks about the gospel he proclaims, which "[God] promised beforehand through his prophets in the holy Scriptures" (v. 2). Next, he quotes an ancient creed, which probably dates back to the Jewish Christian circles in Jerusalem and consists of several Old Testament doctrines (vv. 3–4).[1] As has been mentioned, the theme of Romans also includes the assertion that the proclamation of justification by faith is in line with the Old Testament "as it is written" (vv. 16–17). The argumentation from Scripture continues in every chapter hereafter.

Consequently, primary support for the theme of Romans is provided by Hab. 2:4. The verse may be translated in two ways, depending on whether the expression "by faith" is combined with the subject "the righteous" or with the verb "shall live": either "the righteous by faith shall live" or "the righteous shall live by faith."[2]

In the end, the difference between the two sentences is insignificant, yet the first option corresponds more closely to the assertion that the quote should argue for—namely, that God's righteousness is revealed in the gospel "from faith for faith" (v. 17a). Additionally, at least 3:21–22 and 5:1 refer back to the theme of the epistle, with a clear correlation between "faith" and "righteousness": "the righteousness of God through faith in Jesus Christ for all who believe" (3:22) and "therefore, since we have been justified by faith" (5:1).[3]

It seems that chapters 1–4 provide a detailed explanation of what justification by faith is (the first part of v. 17b: "the righteous [. . .] by faith"), while chapters 5–8 clarify what the eschatological life is like (the second part of v. 17b: "shall live"). Certain lexical data support such a thematic division:

- In 1:18–4:25, the terms πίστις and πιστεύειν are used twenty-nine and eight times, respectively, but in 5:1–8:39, only a few times each.
- In 1:18–4:25, the terms ζωή or ζῆν are used only a few times, but in 5:1–8:39 these terms are used over twenty times altogether.

As stated earlier, theoretically both translations lead to the same theological goal.[4]

The use of Hab. 2:4 as the foundation for defining the theme of Romans works well with the subsequent line of thought. The passage contains two key concepts that reoccur in chapter 4. There Paul similarly quotes an Old Testament passage with the same intent. He refers to Gen. 15:6, which, like Hab. 2:4, speaks of both "faith" and "righteous(ness)." So the argumentation from Scripture in 1:17 leads to the much more thorough exposition of Scripture in 4:1ff. In other words, the definition of the theme and the treatment of the theme correspond exactly.[5]

Obviously, it was first the prophet Habakkuk (and not Paul or someone else) who assumed that the Jews would follow in their fathers' footsteps. Considering the oppression and violence of the Babylonians, Hab. 2:4 appears to treat a similar issue as Gen. 15. In both cases, the people involved face an impossible situation. In addition, it is about their trust in God, who, despite challenging circumstances and many severe obstacles, will intervene in the near future. Interestingly, similar language is used in both cases: "faith," "faithfulness," and "righteous(ness)." In Hebraic context, there is no clear difference—much less a contradiction—between "faith" and "faithfulness." The righteous will save himself from the national catastrophe only through his faith and faithfulness (Hab. 2:4). Likewise, Abraham is declared righteous by his faith (Gen. 15:6) and is then willing, in his faithfulness, to sacrifice his own son Isaac (Gen. 22). In the New Testament, James in particular emphasizes that connection (2:21–24). At its most fundamental level, even Paul's reasoning goes in the same direction. He proclaims justification by faith with the help of Abraham's story (Rom. 4) and admonishes his listeners to present their *own* bodies as "living sacrifice[s], holy and acceptable to God" (Rom. 12:1).[6]

Thus Hab. 2:4 is an excellent summary of the arrangement, structure, and scope of Romans. To be sure, Rom. 1:17 does not misinterpret the purpose and content of the Old Testament quotation. With Israel's ancestor as an example, Habakkuk emphasizes not only faithfulness (obedience toward the law) but also faith. For his part, Paul emphasizes Abraham's faith in Rom. 4 without turning a blind eye to faithfulness. Further evidence for the close connection between Hab. 2:4 and Rom. 1:17 is found in the contexts of both passages thoroughly discussing God's wrath revealed against the ungodliness of mankind (see especially Hab. 3; Rom. 1:18ff.).

Consequently, the authority of Scripture concerns an essential part of the theology of Romans. The gospel flows from the Old Testament. It is intended for "the Jew first and also [. . .] the Greek" (1:16). Next, we proceed further. A more detailed examination of the meaning and use of the arguments from Scripture follows. As with the previous presentation (see chapter 3), the three main divisions of Romans will again be taken into consideration without addressing every Old Testament quote or allusion. That kind of investigation would greatly increase the task at hand. At the outset, with an overall emphasis on chapters 1–8, several general principles will be outlined. Then the focus will turn to chapters 9–11, which contain rich material. Finally, a couple of concrete examples with practical consequences will be studied, especially in light of chapters 12–15. The results will be evaluated in the conclusion.

General Principles

Below, attention will be given to two ways Paul interprets the Old Testament: the "promise-fulfillment" scheme and the typological exposition of Scripture.

(1) The "Promise-Fulfillment" Scheme

Rom. 15:4 will serve as a starting point for the presentation on the fulfillment of the Old Testament promises within the New Testament time span. It states, "For whatever was written in former days was written for our instruction, that through endurance and through the encouragement of the Scriptures we might have hope."

Obviously, "whatever was written in former days" and "Scriptures" are synonymous. So the Old Testament seems to be in its totality a prophecy that concerns us (cf. 1:2). Therefore, it certainly is not even worth our trouble to refute the common misunderstanding that Paul would have only emphasized some significant thoughts in the Old Testament. To read such a modern idea into his texts reveals an anachronistic perspective. Rom. 3:2 most emphatically stresses that the greatest privilege of Jews is that "God's word" (τὰ λόγια, in the plural) had been entrusted to them, not merely some major principles.

The general claim of the benefit of the Scriptures and of their prophetic nature in Rom. 15:4 stresses the Christological application of Ps. 69:10 in the previous verse—that is, in Rom. 15:3: "For Christ did not please himself, but as it is written, 'The reproaches of those who reproached you fell on me.'"

It is a question of the scheme of "promise-fulfillment," something that actually has its place in the intrinsic message of the Old Testament. Rom. 15:8 specifically speaks of the confirmation of "the promises to the patriarchs": "For I tell you that Christ became a servant to the circumcised to show God's truthfulness, in order to confirm the promises given to the patriarchs."

By "the patriarchs" here, Paul means especially the patriarchs Abraham, Isaac, and Jacob but naturally also other great Jewish men. As early as in chapter 4, he takes up the promise that Abraham and his offspring will be "heir[s] of the world" (vv. 13–21). In chapter 9, the apostle then wrestles with the question of the children of the promise: Isaac and Jacob and, in the wake of them, ultimately the Christians (vv. 6–13). He thus explains in the course of the Epistle to the Romans what the confirmation of "the promises to the patriarchs" graphically includes. Second Corinthians 1:20 states programmatically that no matter how many promises God has made, they "find their Yes in him [Christ]."

In line with its theme, the entire Epistle to the Romans deals with one great promise: the revelation of "the righteousness of God, [to which] the Law and the Prophets bear witness" (3:21; cf. Gal. 3, where the promise is identified with justification by faith). Rom. 4 then combines the treatment of the theme with God's promise to Abraham, the Patriarch of the Jews (equally in Gal. 3). When the promises made to the patriarchs resurface in Rom. 9, the connection with chapter 4 is preserved through similar terminology: as Abraham's faith once was "counted" (ἐλογίσθη—λογίζεται) as righteousness to him (see 4:3, 4:5, 4:23–24), now only the children of the promise are "counted" (λογίζεται) as Abraham's offspring (9:8).[7] As a result, we have already gone deeper into what is called typological Bible exposition.[8]

(2) The Typological Exposition of Scripture

Rom. 4:23–24 reassures in regard to the justification of Abraham: "But the words 'it was counted to him' were not written for his sake alone, but for ours also. It will be counted to us who believe in him who raised from the dead Jesus our Lord."

Here we are dealing with "typological" Bible exposition (*typoleges*) with its three main principles:

1. The account or witness of the Old Testament serves as a "prototype" (*typos*) of what is going to come in the days of "fulfillment" (*antitypos*).
2. The later salvation event rises above the previous—that is, the *antitypos* is superior to the *typos*.
3. The deepest content of the Old Testament is understood only through the gospel, in and through faith in Christ, and it specifically deals with the Christians.

Typological Bible exposition always emerges from the clear significance of the Old Testament text and applies it to the real situation in the church. The thought that God remains the same and acts in the same way underlies such a method. The earlier saving deeds therefore anticipate the ones to come. The Old Testament already uses typological Bible exposition. For instance, Isaiah compares Israel's return from exile with creation or the Exodus (Isa. 43:1–7, 14–21).

An equal example appears in Rom. 9, where the typological interpretation is utilized in a passage that again comes out of the account of Abraham. There the focus lies on his two sons: just as only Isaac's descendants were counted as Abraham's offspring, so now the children of the promise alone are counted as God's family (vv. 6–9): "This means that it is not the children of the flesh who are the children of God, but the children of the promise are counted as offspring" (v. 8).

It is not only a similarity but also a dissimilarity that is explained by *typos*. Rom. 5 talks about Adam as Christ's "prototype" (v. 14: τύπος), but later on *contrasts* existing between them are described (vv. 15–19).[9]

Equally, *typos* can function as a negative prototype. With a typological intent, 1 Cor. 10 tells about Israel's wandering in the wilderness. The nation's apostasy and sins of different kinds serve as "warning" examples (v. 11: τυπικῶς) for Christians.[10]

On the contrary, allegorical interpretation seems totally arbitrary. It is seldom employed by the New Testament authors and even then in combination with typological Bible exposition (see Gal. 4:24–26). Paul's method of arguing can be contrasted with Philo, who most often uses allegory without any consideration of the actual meaning of the text.[11]

(3) A Christological Reading of the Old Testament

So the two main principles for Paul's interpretation of the Old Testament—that is, the "promise-fulfillment" scheme and the typological Bible exposition—appear in his treatment of the Abraham narratives (chapters 4 and 9), which no doubt hold a central position in the Epistle to the Romans. It sounds as if his entire study of the Old Testament is leavened by such a double perspective. Everything revolves around Christ: he fulfills the promises, and he unlocks the typological meaning of the Scriptures.

In light of the reality that God is and remains faithful and fulfills all his promises, and in view of the fact that he is the same and acts the same way in both the old and new covenants, the entire Old Testament emerges as a Christological book with an eschato-logical message.[12] Accordingly, there are not merely some sporadic prophecies about the Messiah. Instead, every single writing turns into a prophetic text about him. Examining the holy revelation in this way does not impose strange and irrelevant categories onto it. On the contrary, history is always to be understood only in hind-sight. The unfolding of salvation history reaches its climax in Christ. He articulates how the past draws attention to and finds its conclu-sion precisely in him. The profound connection between the old and new covenants becomes lucid when it is elucidated through the gospel. In other words: Romans advocates not an *anachronistic* but a *diachronic* (historic) perspective.[13]

With the general principles for a Pauline understanding of Scripture as a starting point, a more in-depth study of the argumen-tation in Rom. 9–11 follows. In line with the definition of the task at hand, numerous Old Testament quotes in particular will be given special attention.[14]

Focus on Rom. 9–11

(1) Prologue

In chapters 9–11, Paul continues his examination of the epistle's theme (1:16–17): if his gospel is truly meant "to the Jew first and also to the Greek," why did Israel not receive it? His gospel has been "the power of God for salvation" mostly among the Gentiles but not so much among Jews. It sounds strange that God's own people would not care about God's revelation.[15] And if that is the case, what has happened to his covenant faithfulness? Has he himself rejected his people and broken his promises? Ultimately, chapters 9–11 deal with God's righteousness (truthfulness or trustworthiness) as much as Israel's righteousness (salvation). The two aspects go together and complete each other, an important fact that should be regarded more seriously when discussing the structure of Romans (see, e.g., 1:16–17, 3:3–8, 3:25–26; cf. my treatment of chapters 9–11 below).[16]

Further, Paul responds to accusations against him. Who knows if he—the notorious apostle to the Gentiles—in his fervor to preach the law-free gospel, is to be blamed for the failed mission to the Jews! In addition, some members of the church in Rome are showing contempt toward the Jewish people and pride in themselves (11:13–32), which creates even more disunion and confusion.[17]

Hence chapters 9–11 have a direct connection to the main argumentation throughout Romans. They do not deviate from the context or form an excursus. The main question is whether Israel, because of her stubbornness, has completely lost her position as God's chosen people and been replaced by the Gentile Christians. Although Paul wrestles with the questions of theodicy, predestination, free will, and salvation history, none of those issues should be seen as an all-encompassing subject matter of the text. They and other secondary investigations, relevant as they may be, necessarily lead to the conclusion that his treatise in chapters 9–11 forms an excursus in Romans.[18]

In view of due consideration given to the position of Israel, it appears fully understandable that the apostle quotes the Old Testament frequently in Rom. 9–11. Almost one-third of all his quotations are found in those three chapters. His entire argument hinges on showing the intimate connection between the gospel and Holy Scriptures. By and large, even Israel's current stubbornness has been foretold by the prophets, who foresaw her unbelief in the coming Messiah. Thus the apostle stands on the biblical basis. He is not like the later heretic Marcion, who dared to completely reject the earlier revelation.[19]

The somewhat hard criticism of Israel's impenitence, which Rom. 9–11 (as well as the interpretation below) exposes, is not to be labeled as anti-Semitism. That concept presupposes a race ideology that is completely foreign to the New Testament (and equally to the Old Testament). Furthermore, it seems hardly fair to view the Pauline presentation as an anti-Jewish contribution to the discussion. At that time, Judaism was not yet one fixed "normative religion." There were several variations, of which the Christian movement was an important one. Paul never truly abandoned his mother religion. He was and remained a Jew among Jews. It is also worth noting that the argumentation in chapters 9–11 culminates in 11:25–27, a prophecy about a marvelous future for *all* of Israel, her coming glorious salvation. Besides, the passage is preceded by vv. 17–24, where some Gentile Christians are admonished for their pride toward the Israelites (see below).[20]

Rom. 9–11 has a quite simple and clear structure. The framework is a lament over Israel in the beginning (9:1–5) and a doxology to God in the end (11:33–36).[21] Rom. 9:6 begins with the main statement "But it is not as though the word of God has failed." Next, the demonstration of reasons for that continues through v. 29 (or maybe even to the last verses of chapter 11).[22] Then subsequently, every pericope begins with a rhetorical question (9:30, 11:1, 11:11) and ends with several Old Testament quotes (10:18–21, 11:8–10, 11:26b–27; see also 9:25–29). Accordingly, the other units are 9:30–10:21, 11:1–10, and 11:11–32.[23]

Below, all the passages are studied one by one.

(2) 9:1–5

To begin with, Paul emphasizes his strong solidarity with the people of Israel and his great faithfulness toward its holy traditions.[24] His gospel does not cause the "word of God"—that is, the Old Testament—to fail (see v. 6). Such a thought is far from him.

The apostle's wish for himself to be accursed in the place of his brothers (v. 3) corresponds to Moses's desire to be blotted out of the book of life together with his countrymen (Exod. 32:30–32).[25] His assurance that he will speak the truth and not lie (v. 1)[26] functions as a solemn oath, which—according to ancient custom—is reinforced by the promise to bring death down upon oneself. It could be that the reference to Christ and the Holy Spirit (v. 1) in that case conforms to the requirement of "two or three witnesses" (see, e.g., Deut. 17:6, 19:15).[27] It is not difficult to find parallels in the life of Moses to the sorrow and agony constantly afflicting Paul in his heart (v. 2). They both suffer much because of their divine callings.[28]

From the outset, Paul acts as a true prophet, who reproaches Israel for transgressions and apostasy yet gives hope for the future if they repent (cf. the many critical statements in chaps. 9–11 with "revealing of the mystery of God" in 11:25ff.).[29] He represents, as it were, the messengers of the old covenant, but his message is far greater: it is the fulfillment of all of their writings.

Hence Paul himself exemplifies the leading principle in the Jewish interpretation of Scripture that the Law of Moses is to be explained with help from the prophets, a method he uses, for example, in 9:12–13 and 10:19–21 (see below). He embodies some characteristics of the spiritual calling of Moses and the prophets.[30]

Next, Paul begins enumerating the indisputable privileges of Israel compared to other people of the world (vv. 4–5) with the Holy Scripture as his starting point. Here he actually continues the enumeration he interrupted in chapter 3. Already there, it was his intention to point out the advantages of the Jews (v. 1), but he settles for only πρῶτον ("first") affirming that they "were entrusted with the oracles of God" (v. 2). In that context, there is no further account. The reader must wait until chapter 9 in order to learn more. At long last, he is told.[31]

Interestingly, τὰ λόγια τοῦ θεοῦ ("the very words of God") mentioned in 3:2 are missing in 9:4–5. It appears as if Paul now enumerates the privileges that the Holy Scripture testifies about (see below). He then develops his reasoning in the beginning of the following section and underscores that ὁ λόγος τοῦ θεοῦ ("the word of God") cannot fail (v. 6), a thesis that refers back in particular to the privileges just enumerated (vv. 4–5). Consequently, chapters 3 and 9 have a deep foundational connection to each other.[32]

What are the privileges asserted in vv. 4–5 that Israel owns according to the Old Testament? The first sentence, οἵτινές εἰσιν Ἰσραηλεῖται ("they are Israelites" in v. 4), functions as a heading. It is important to note that in chapters 9–11, Paul no longer speaks about the Jews but about Israelites. So his unbelieving countrymen still bear that honorary name. God has not rejected his people, even if most of them have forsaken the gospel (11:1; see also v. 28). His word has not lost its validity for them, constituting what is demonstrably a central thought to the whole argument.[33]

The following account of Israel's privileges (vv. 4–5) consists of three parts:

a. "Theirs is (ὧν) . . ." (two feminine singular nouns + one feminine plural noun, twice)

> b. "Theirs are (ὧν) . . ." (only one masculine plural noun,
>   which is therefore separated from the previous)
> c. "From them (ἐξ ὧν) . . ."[34]

The structure is framed by reference to the natural lineage (v. 3: "my kinsmen according to the flesh"; v. 5: their Messiah "according to the flesh").[35]

In consideration of the whole structure, first the *Israelites* (heading) are mentioned, and a number of their various privileges are accounted (point *a*). Then follows *the patriarchs*, central figures in salvation history (point *b*). Finally, the focus rests on *the Messiah*, "who is God over all"[36] (point *c*). Evidently, the direction is from a multitude to a single one (or the only one).[37] Further, the account of Israel's privileges contains only evidence of grace given. None of them results from gaining exceptional merits or earning a special status. What do they stand for?

Point *a* above (v. 4) recounts most of the privileges:[38]

- υἱοθεσία ("adoption"): Israel is God's son
- δόξα ("glory"): God's presence (the Old Testament: *kabod*; rabbinism: *shekina)* first and foremost in the temple
- διαθῆκαι ("the covenants"): God's covenants with Abraham, Isaac, Jacob, Moses, David, and so on
- νομοθεσία ("the law"): as it was given by God, but not its negative consequences because of sin's dominion (see, e.g., chapter 7)
- λατρεία ("the worship"): worship in the temple
- ἐπαγγελίαι ("the promises"): especially the promises to the patriarchs (see already chapter 4)[39]

Point *b* (v. 5a) above adds only one privilege: πατέρες ("the patriarchs")—not only Abraham, Isaac, and Jacob but also other forefathers.[40]

Points *a* and *b* (together with 3:2) include as good as all of Israel's privileges except two: the Messiah and God. They are mentioned in point *c* (v. 5b).

The change in the wording ("from them" instead of "theirs") reveals that the Israelites, despite all their privileges, do not live in a close saving relationship with their Messiah or God. On the contrary, they have rejected him.[41]

For certain, a close connection between the Messiah and God prevails in v. 5, but how do they relate to each other? There are at least three main alternatives to translate the last sentence, ὁ Χριστὸς τὸ κατὰ σάρκα, ὁ ὢν ἐπὶ πάντων Θεὸς εὐλογητὸς εἰς τοὺς αἰῶνας:

a. "The Christ according to the flesh, who is God over all, blessed forever. Amen."
b. "The Christ according to the flesh, who is over all. God, be blessed forever. Amen."
c. "The Christ according to the flesh. God, who is over all, be blessed forever. Amen."[42]

The main question is whether Christ is called "God."

Without a shred of doubt, it seems most natural to understand the doxology in v. 5 as an apposition to Christ (i.e., option *a* above) for the following reasons:

a. In other contexts the relative clause "who is . . ." also refers back to the previous subject.
b. Doxologies in the Pauline Epistles are directly connected to the previous clause.
c. The Jewish expression "blessed be" occurs in the beginning of a clause (an exception is LXX Ps. 67:19: κύριος ὁ θεός εὐλογητός), not in the middle of the sentence as it is here.
d. The expression τὸ κατὰ σάρκα ("according to the flesh") implies an antithesis (cf. 1:3–4) and presupposes "something more."[43]

In addition to the former mainly structural reasons, the theological argument might prove most convincing:

e. Consistent with a good literary style, the greatest privilege was to be mentioned last as a climax—in this case, Israel's God. Thus it does not seem likely that the long list would be interrupted after mentioning the Christ (Messiah). No, God is in fact the God of the *Jews* (cf., e.g., 3:29 or the well-known introductory clause in Jewish doxologies: "Blessed are You, Lord *our* God"), and he has revealed himself in Jesus of Nazareth. It follows that the Jews who reject their Messiah then reject their own God. Consequently, there is a serious threat hidden behind vv. 4–5, which sheds more light on the grief in v. 2 also.[44]

In view of vv. 1–5, Paul strives for showing from the outset that his gospel conforms to Israel's unique status and special revelation. He does not abolish Jewish tradition insofar as it originates from the Old Testament and brings glory to the Messiah—that is, Yahweh.[45]

(3) 9:6-29

The whole passage deals with and defends the following thesis in v. 6a:

Οὐχ οἷον δὲ ὅτι ἐκπέπτωκεν ὁ λόγος τοῦ Θεοῦ.

But it is not as though the word of God has failed.[46]

On account of the connection between the Messiah and God (v. 5, see above), such a programmatic sentence means that the Scriptures speak about Jesus Christ or, perhaps better, that Christ has spoken and still speaks in the Scriptures. In that case, Paul means that the Christological interpretation of the Old Testament is the hermeneutical key to his understanding of revelation, which, indeed, is what he points out in the following verses.[47]

The thesis in v. 6a demands an illustrative overview of biblical history or at least some definite pieces of evidence that show that God's word has not in fact failed.[48] That explains the extensive use of various Old Testament passages in the following survey.[49] The thorough argumentation follows the canonical order quite well: first Genesis, then Exodus, and finally (and also in between) the prophets.[50] By and large, the rationale draws upon the Old Testament view of Yahweh as *Israel's* God. But if he no longer wants to be Israel's God, he has broken his promises and forsaken his word—a looming problem for the Early Church, which originates from Judaism. Does the gospel proclaim another God, who cannot be identified with Israel's God? The answer lies in vv. 6b–29.[51]

A key word that unites the argumentation in the passage and serves as a link between several Old Testament references is the verb κάλειν (to "call" or "count" in vv. 7, 12, 24–26). It does not denote a general invitation but expresses the initiative and active intervention of the Creator, who cares for his people (see already, e.g., 4:17). Salvation is based not on their merits but on his grace alone. Moreover, in most of the quotations, the divine "I" occurs (ἐγώ and verbs only in first-person singular), which puts more emphasis on God's free and sovereign choice of grace.[52] Considering vv. 6–29, a calling from him is needed—a Jewish lineage does not guarantee that an Israelite belongs to the true Israel![53]

Paul begins his brief overview of biblical history with two similar examples in vv. 7–9 and 10–13. In both cases, he quotes the Old Testament twice and pits two brothers against each other (Isaac and Ismael, Jacob and Esau). Further, both cases concern Jewish patriarchs and their birth narratives. Verses 10–13 go a bit further than vv. 7–9 by drawing attention to the difference that Isaac (Sarah's son) and Ismael (Hagar's son) were not born of the same mother, while Jacob and Esau as twin brothers did have Rebecca as their mother.[54]

Based on the argumentation of vv. 7–9, it seems as if the promise definitely is for Isaac and all his descendants, but in line with vv. 10–13, another surprising limitation occurs already in the next generation when the blessing is confined to Jacob and his descendants. A very similar development has taken place and continues to do so over time. Verse 29 then foresees further limitations and refers to Isa. 1:9, which predicts,

Εἰ μὴ Κύριος Σαβαὼθ ἐγκατέλιπεν ἡμῖν σπέρμα, ὡς Σόδομα ἂν ἐγενήθημεν καὶ ὡς Γόμορρα ἂν ὡμοιώθημεν.

If the Lord of hosts had not left us offspring (descendants), we would have been like Sodom and become like Gomorrah.

The quotation follows LXX verbatim without any changes.

By and large, the entire Old Testament aims at telling how Yahweh gradually particularizes his promise regarding the so-called seed of the woman (Gen. 3:15) and how he constantly guards and fulfills his word by rejecting those who do not submit to him in faith and faithfulness. Thus Paul develops his thoughts in vv. 6–29 from a main plot firmly consistent with the Old Testament. His overview of biblical history cuts directly to the red thread in Holy Scripture (cf. also 11:1ff. below).[55]

Without a doubt, the argumentation in vv. 7–13 uses a typological exposition of Scripture with an application to the New Testament context.[56] The notion of being born fits well with the question about salvation, since neither presupposes a person's own merits. This becomes especially clear in the narrative of Isaac's conception and birth:

Τοῦτ' ἔστιν, οὐ τὰ τέκνα τῆς σαρκός, ταῦτα τέκνα τοῦ θεοῦ· ἀλλὰ τὰ τέκνα τῆς ἐπαγγελίας λογίζεται εἰς σπέρμα.

This means that it is not the children of the flesh who are the children of God, but the children of the promise are counted as offspring. (v. 8)

In accordance with the Old Testament events foreshadowing the future, the Gentile Christians—namely, the Christian church in general—represented by "the younger brother," now have priority over Israel, represented by "the older brother." The Christians alone are counted as heirs of all the promises in the past. Their new, special position is not based on any kind of unfairness. The Israelites themselves had been favored previously (albeit "according to the flesh"), "the younger brother" (Isaac and Jacob) over "the older brother" (Ismael and Esau). Their privileges and unique status have derived from God's wise counsel and guidance regarding salvation history. He still remains free to act in as sovereign a way as before (see primarily vv. 11–12).[57] Therefore, from the perspective of the

New Testament, the typological reading of the Old Testament surprisingly enough reveals that the Israelites are now identified as the descendants of Ismael and Esau. It must have sounded very harsh to them.[58]

As a result, υἱοθεσία ("the adoption") in v. 4 should not be understood as an *ethnic* privilege or a *birthright*. The Greek term assumes that someone is explicitly "counted" (λογίζεται) as Abraham's and God's child (vv. 7–8) just as the godless man in chapter 4 is counted as righteous by faith. Therefore, also the Jews, who are Abraham's children "according to the flesh," must be adopted in order to become children of God "in the Spirit."[59] "What counts […] is grace, not race."[60]

To confirm God's sovereign counsel and guidance in salvation history, an embarrassing text from Mal. 1:2–3 is quoted in v. 13. It serves to interpret one passage in the Torah, "the older shall serve the younger" (Gen. 25:23, which is quoted in v. 12), with the help of the prophets in accordance with Jewish custom (see above).[61] The quotation both ends the previous pericope and begins the next:

Τὸν Ἰακὼβ ἠγάπησα, τὸν δὲ Ἠσαῦ ἐμίσησα.

Jacob I loved, but Esau I hated.

LXX: καὶ ἠγάπησα τὸν Ιακωβ, τὸν δὲ Ησαυ ἐμίσησα.

The verb "hate" is in the aorist form (ἐμίσησα) and in Greek may express a one-time event. Hence to "hate Esau" does not necessarily indicate a perpetual status (however, cf. Heb. 12:16–17).[62] On the other hand, the verb "hate" is the opposite of "love" (ἠγάπησα, also aorist), which is further parallel with "choose" (κάλειν in v. 12). Thus it seems slightly more likely that the quotation in v. 13 testifies to a clear-cut distinction between Jacob and Esau, which has its deepest foundation in God's merciful election. Besides, later in Mal. 1:4, Edom (= Esau) is called "the people with whom the LORD is angry forever."[63] Instead of being offended by the almost fatalistic thought and anxiously asking why God hated Esau (who, however, in several instances showed his weak character and corruption), one may just as well marvel at the abundant grace and with astonishment ask why God loved Jacob (who was not in any way better than his brother and supposedly an even greater sinner). To consider along those lines helps avoid the dangers of a false doctrine of predestination.[64]

As a result, the question in v. 14 easily arises:

Τί οὖν ἐροῦμεν; μὴ ἀδικία παρὰ τῷ θεῷ;

What shall we say then? Is there injustice on God's part?

For certain, the question is answered with a resounding μὴ γένοιτο ("By no means!"). The following verses give the motivation for the answer in two identical arrangements:

No,
v. 15: for Scripture says . . . (quotation from Ex. 33:19),
v. 16: so . . . (the conclusion drawn from the quotation).[65]

No,
v. 17: for Scripture says . . . (quotation from Ex. 9:16),
v. 18: so . . . (the conclusion drawn from the quotation).[66]

Not only that, but the argumentation in vv. 15–16 explains the first part of the quotation in v. 13 ("Jacob I loved"), while the argumentation in vv. 17–18 explains the second part of the quotation in v. 13 ("Esau I hated").[67]

Even if the limits of the current work prohibit a deeper look into the church's (or churches') doctrines of predestination,[68] it is worth noting the apostolic way of arguing: Scripture is carefully explained with Scripture. What is more, the biblical narrative about Pharaoh's hardness of heart (vv. 17–18) shows that even negative events in salvation history, at least at times, have positive consequences—in this case that God's name "might be proclaimed in all the earth" (v. 17). Consequently, Israel's current hardness of heart has caused the gospel to be proclaimed for all Gentiles throughout the world (11:11–15).[69] By such a typological exposition, her own fate is—somewhat surprisingly—likened to the destiny of Egypt, in accordance with the earlier accounts of Ismael (vv. 6–9) and Esau (vv. 10–13).[70]

Verse 19 continues the line of thought with a new objection:

Ἐρεῖς μοι οὖν Τί ἔτι μέμφεται; τῷ γὰρ βουλήματι αὐτοῦ τίς ἀνθέστηκεν;

You will say to me then, "Why does he still find fault? For who can resist his will?"[71]

The questions are not answered instantly. Instead, v. 20 asks a counter-question beginning with the contrast between man (the first word in the clause) and God (the last word in the clause): ὦ ἄνθρωπε, μενοῦνγε σὺ τίς εἶ ὁ ἀνταποκρινόμενος τῷ Θεῷ; ("who are you, O man, to answer back to God?")[72] Then the focus lies on the example of the potter who forms the clay into a pot—without a word of explanation (vv. 20b–23). The metaphor obviously refers to God as the Creator. He has created man from the dust of the earth (Gen. 2:7). The Old Testament often uses that kind of imagery (see especially Isa. 29:16, 45:9; cf. furthermore 64:8; Jer. 18:1–6; Wisd. 15:7). With such a theological perspective as a starting point, the Creator cannot be held accountable for anything before the world. Indeed, he has the right of "self-realization," so to speak. No one should make claims to him (see more closely the book of Job).[73] Still, the truth of God's sovereignty does not mean that he acts arbitrarily. Paul formulates his text with judgment. He writes of σκεύη ὀργῆς (the "vessels of wrath") that they are κατηρτισμένα ("prepared for destruction" in v. 22)—in other words, that their possible devastation is not explicitly connected to God's predestination. But of σκεύη ἐλέους (the "vessels of mercy"), he writes that God has "prepared beforehand for glory" (ἃ προητοίμασεν εἰς δόξαν in v. 23)—in other words, that their coming glory is based only on God's gracious election (however, cf. v. 18).[74] At large, there is no necessity of continuing to discuss predestination further here. The difference between passive and active voice in vv. 22–23 must suffice.[75]

In consequence, Paul treats the issue of theodicy (v. 14) not with the help of rationalism or logic but according to the testimony of Scripture (vv. 15–18) and the reality of creation (vv. 20–23). Surely he is no philosopher but a serious theologian! God's actions are in line with his revelation and own essence as the origin of the universe. Only at that rate does faith in his absolute goodness hold even in the midst of chaos, which is characterized by a completely incomprehensible course of events.[76]

In direct connection to v. 23, v. 24 emphasizes that God has called the "vessels of mercy" (v. 23) "not from the Jews only but also from the Gentiles" (v. 24),[77] according to the standard Jewish view all Gentiles were to remain "vessels of wrath" forever. Yet now they have become part of salvation through the gospel. They have been granted entrance into God's own people. Most Jews, though, have been excluded. Because of their unbelief, they no longer have the right to count themselves as "vessels of mercy." On the contrary, in context, it turns out that to a great extent the "vessels of wrath" coincide with Israel "according to the flesh." Salvation history has again been turned upside down, as has been shown in the narratives of Ismael, Esau, and Pharaoh (see above)![78]

The next series of quotes in vv. 25–29 explains more in-depth the sentence "not from the Jews only but also from the Gentiles" in the form a chiasm (A-B-B-A):[79]

A God has called the Jews (v. 24),
B God has called the Gentiles (v. 24),
B′ The Old Testament confirms point B (vv. 25–26),
A′ The Old Testament confirms point A (vv. 27–29).

Here Hosea 2:23 and 1:10 are quoted in vv. 25–26, and Isaiah 10:22–23 and 1:9 in vv. 27–29.[80]

To begin with the quotation from Hosea in vv. 25–26 (for the combination of the original texts of LXX, see the discussion below),

Καλέσω τὸν οὐ λαόν μου λαόν μου καὶ τὴν οὐκ ἠγαπημένην ἠγαπημένην·
Καὶ ἔσται, ἐν τῷ τόπῳ οὗ ἐρρήθη αὐτοῖς, Οὐ λαός μου ὑμεῖς, ἐκεῖ κληθήσονται υἱοὶ θεοῦ ζῶντος.

Those who were not my people I will call "my people," and her who was not beloved I will call "beloved."

And in the very place where it was said to them, "You are not my people," there they will be called "sons of the living God."

In its original context, Hosea speaks about *Israel's* future lot, but now his prophecy is overtly applied to the *Gentiles'* situation (cf. further 1 Pet. 2:10). What lies behind such a radical change of perspective? Many different explanations have been presented within New Testament research, and they are not to be dealt with here.[81] The following is the author's own view.

Chapter 11 demonstrates that the apostle does keep in mind the original sense and content of the prophetic accounts: Israel, who is now Lo-Ammi ("not my people"), will in the future again be called Ammi ("my people"). This eschatological aspect appears especially clearly in vv. 25–26 (cf. also vv. 11–16, 23–24, 30–32).[82] In the same chapter, Israel is likened to the true olive tree (vv. 17–24), metaphorical language that has its origin not least in Hosea (14:7). Unhappily, a large amount of the branches have been cut off because of unbelief (cf. Jer. 11:16, which instead speaks about burning the branches).[83] No doubt, they refer to Jews who have rejected their Messiah. In their place, branches of a wild olive tree—against their nature—have been grafted, and they share the true olive tree's nutritious root. The description fits the Gentiles well. They now have the right to join Israel. The privileges of the chosen people belong to them in faith. Therefore, Hosea's prophecies speak to them and about them. His visions are actualized in a surprising way in different circumstances, which Paul strives to come to grips with from his New Testament perspective. Ultimately, his exposition of Scripture is not at variance with the meaning that is initially included in the Old Testament text.[84]

Moreover, Hosea 1:10 (LXX 2:1) begins with a conventional prophecy that ὁ ἀριθμὸς τῶν υἱῶν Ισραηλ ὡς ἡ ἄμμος τῆς θαλάσσης, ἣ οὐκ ἐκμετρηθήσεται οὐδὲ ἐξαριθμηθήσεται ("the number of the children of Israel shall be like the sand of the sea, which cannot be measured or numbered"). The prediction about an incalculable amount of Israelites unequivocally refers back to the promise to Abraham: in the future, his descendants will be like "the sand of the sea," which cannot be counted (Gen. 22:17, 32:12; cf. also 13:16, 15:5; Exod. 32:13; 1 Kings 4:20; Heb. 11:12), and he himself will be a "father of a multitude of nations" (Gen. 17:5). According to Rom. 4, all of this has really been fulfilled through the gospel, which is directed not only to the Jews but also to Gentiles (especially vv. 16–18, where the preceding promises in Genesis are explicitly quoted). Hence Hosea 1:10 must refer to Gentiles as well. The broader "canonical" context logically leads to that conclusion. For sure, Paul has noted the first sentence of Hosea 1:10, since he reads the expression "the number of the children of Israel" into his next quote, Isa. 10:22 (v. 27, see below).[85]

Paul then proceeds and addresses Israel's spiritual state in vv. 27–28 with the help of Isa. 10:22–23 (for the modification of the original text of LXX, see the discussion below):

Ἐὰν ᾖ ὁ ἀριθμὸς τῶν υἱῶν Ἰσραὴλ ὡς ἡ ἄμμος τῆς θαλάσσης, τὸ ὑπόλειμμα σωθήσεται· λόγον γὰρ συντελῶν καὶ συντέμνων ποιήσει Κύριος ἐπὶ τῆς γῆς.

Though the number of the sons of Israel be as the sand of the sea, only a remnant of them will be saved, for the Lord will carry out his sentence upon the earth fully and without delay. (vv. 27b–28)[86]

The quotation is drawn upon in a very unusual way. It says that Ἡσαΐας δὲ κράζει ὑπὲρ τοῦ Ἰσραήλ ("Isaiah cries out concerning Israel") in v. 27a. The conspicuous language seems to assume that God's Spirit is at work in his prophet. Rom. 8:15 and Gal. 4:6 mention how Christians in the Spirit cry out (or the Spirit in the Christians cries out), "Abba! Father!" The similarity is obvious.[87] Furthermore, the language certainly expresses anguish and sorrow connected to Israel's spiritual state also. Most of her children will perish. What a catastrophe![88]

Moreover, Paul combines the quotation from Isaiah with the previous quotation from Hosea in a masterful way. He substitutes ὁ λαὸς Ἰσραήλ ("your people Israel") in Isa. 10:22 with another formulation, ὁ ἀριθμὸς τῶν υἱῶν Ἰσραήλ ("the number of the children of Israel"), stemming from Hosea 1:10, which is precisely the text quoted in v. 26! Besides, it is worth observing that both Isa. 10:22 and Hosea 1:10 liken the Israelites to ἡ ἄμμος τῆς θαλάσσης ("the sand of the sea"), which provides yet one more connection between the two.

With such linguistic meanings in his reasoning, Paul suggests that his sources truly speak about the same state of affairs in concert, thus demonstrating the unity of the Old Testament witnesses.[89]

Even though Isa. 22b–23 is paraphrased quite a lot in v. 28, its main content is nevertheless preserved. It speaks of the definiteness and finality in God's judgment (cf. the later historical development up until AD 70). The two participles συντελῶν and συντέμνων together make up an idiomatic expression that is not possible to translate literally. The ESV renders it "fully and without delay," interpreting it to refer to God's "sentence upon the earth."[90] To be precise, the Greek text, however, is speaking of λόγος ("the word"), not "sentence." In that case, v. 28 refers back to v. 6, which initiates the whole section with the main thesis that ὁ λόγος τοῦ θεοῦ ("God's word") cannot fail. As determined by ancient style and rhetoric, after the treatment of the theme, a summary generally follows just as it has here. Verse 28 ends the long line of reasoning with repetition and clarification of the subject matter (*inclusio*).[91] For that reason, the Greek could be translated literally: "The Lord will carry out his word (of promise) fulfilling and shortening on earth." The first participle, "fulfilling," underlines that the Lord performs his promises. His word never fails (v. 6a). The second participle, "shortening," underscores that the Lord will still judge those who do not trust in him. His word stands firm despite their stubbornness (especially vv. 6b–13), which inevitably causes the number saved to be considerably reduced (see v. 27). Put differently, God's word continually prevails (v. 6a, the "qualitative" aspect), but "not all who are descended from Israel belong to Israel" (v. 6b, the "quantitative" aspect).[92]

In agreement with vv. 27–28, v. 29 emphasizes the main point using another passage from Isaiah (1:9):

Εἰ μὴ Κύριος Σαβαώθ ἐγκατέλιπεν ἡμῖν σπέρμα, ὡς Σόδομα ἂν ἐγενήθημεν καὶ ὡς Γόμορρα ἂν ὡμοιώθημεν.

Unless the Lord Almighty had left us descendants, we would have been like Sodom and become like Gomorrah.

LXX: Καὶ εἰ μὴ κύριος σαβαωθ ἐγκατέλιπεν ἡμῖν σπέρμα, ὡς Σοδομα ἂν ἐγενήθημεν καὶ ὡς Γομορρα ἂν ὡμοιώθημεν.

Once more, the key argument of the chapter is confirmed—namely, that God only chooses a part of Israel as his spiritual people. Yet he does leave "us descendants." Verse 29 returns to the question of a remnant discussed already in vv. 6b–9 and summarizes the whole study.[93]

Finally, it may be added that the Pauline idea of a remnant gains weighty support in Isaiah's prophetic proclamation. In his time, the worldwide political situation was very tense. Assyria threatened all of the Middle East. Slowly, nation after nation was conquered, and soon it was Judah's turn. Isaiah prophesies that "the waters of the River, mighty and many"—in other words, the king of Assyria—will "sweep on into Judah, [and] it will overflow and pass on, reaching even to the neck" (8:7–8). Only the head—that is, the capital, Jerusalem—will be spared (see 7:8–9 for similar language, where "the head of Aram" is Damascus and "the head of Ephraim" is Samaria). Yet in a decisive moment, the Lord intervenes. He saves Zion through a great miracle (see especially chapter 37, where "the angel of the Lord" destroys the Assyrian army) because a righteous king, Immanuel, rules there (Isa. 7:14). It seems that the prophecy refers to Hezekiah as a type for the Messiah (cf. 8:8 against the historical background in chapter 37 and quite unmistakable allusions to the meaning of Immanuel in 2 Chron. 32:7–8).[94] Regarding that critical time, 1:8, among other passages, prophesies as follows:

Ἐγκαταλειφθήσεται ἡ θυγάτηρ Σιων ὡς σκηνὴ ἐν ἀμπελῶνι καὶ ὡς ὀπωροφυλάκιον ἐν σικυηράτῳ, ὡς πόλις πολιορκουμένη·

And the daughter of Zion is left like a booth in a vineyard, like a lodge in a cucumber field, like a besieged city.

Then the following verse is quoted in Rom. 9:29.[95] Apparently, Paul assumes that Israel lives again in the middle of a serious crisis that threatens her existence. Only a small remnant will be rescued, yet in the end, "all Israel" will be saved thanks to the righteous King (Savior), who comes "from Zion" (11:26; see below).[96]

In summary, the theological interpretation in 9:6–29 is based on a typological reading of Scripture and includes two specific biblical motifs: the prophecies about the "seed" (offspring) and the imagery about the Creator as the Potter. Both are very prominent theological aspects of the Old Testament. Hence the interpretation is about not a few loose details or subtleties but the core message of Scripture.

Still, how did this come about that Israel "according to the flesh" represents Ismael, Esau, Pharaoh, or "vessels of wrath" (9:6–29)? This rather shocking turning point in the history of salvation is more thoroughly explained in 9:30–10:21.

(4) 9:30–10:21

The pericope begins with further accounts of various perspectives on the salvation of the Gentiles and Jews. The former have obtained righteousness by faith (9:30). The latter, however, imagine that they attain righteousness on account of their works and have therefore completely missed their goal. They have stumbled over the stumbling stone, which is the Messiah (9:31–33). The argumentation continues in chapter 10 with the same intent and ends in a similar way to the beginning—that is, with a critique of Israel's fall (*inclusio*: cf. 9:31–33, 10:19–21, to each other).[97]

The phrase διώκων νόμον δικαιοσύνης ("pursue a *law of righteousness*" in 9:31) should not be thoughtlessly translated or understood as if the Jews simply pursued the *righteousness of the law*. Rather, it suggests that they were interested in the right interpretation of the law, which alone guarantees complete righteousness before God. Therefore, they had very complicated *halakic* discussions on many subjects (explanations of the Mosaic instructions).[98] The right "practice" (*orthopraxis*) assumes right "knowledge" (*orthodoxy*). Even the rich man in Mark 10:17 (par.) wants to *ask* and *know* what he needs to *do* "to inherit eternal life." His fervor and enthusiasm truly illustrate what "pursuing a law of righteousness" means.[99]

Despite a sincere goal, the Jewish zeal for the law falls short. It is a failure from the beginning. Righteousness cannot be attained by works. It does not exist anywhere else but in the Messiah, Christ. He is called "the LORD [. . .] our righteousness" (Jer. 23:6, 33:16). In agreement with this, two Messianic prophecies from Isaiah (8:14; 28:16) are quoted and combined in v. 33. They both mention "the stone":[100]

Ἰδοὺ τίθημι ἐν Σιὼν λίθον προσκόμματος καὶ πέτραν σκανδάλου, καὶ ὁ πιστεύων ἐπ᾽ αὐτῷ οὐ καταισχυνθήσεται.

Behold, I am laying in Zion a stone of stumbling, and a rock of offense; and whoever believes in him will not be put to shame.[101]

The same combination appears in 1 Pet. 2:6–8 and is assumed in Luke 2:34. Thus it represents an original Christian scriptural argument directed at false expectations for the Messiah.[102]

The quote or quotes in v. 33 should not be misinterpreted so that they would direct attention *exclusively* toward a Christological misjudgment.[103] Especially in light of the context, the emphasis lies also on an anthropological mistake. Both aspects are closely connected. In other words, Paul criticizes the Jews not simply because they do not believe in Christ but rather because they do not believe in Christ due to their trust in their own righteousness. Yet since this issue has already received sufficient attention in other contexts, it will not be explored further here.[104]

Moreover, v. 33 confirms that the gospel is not at odds with the Old Testament or the promise to Abraham (see above). On the contrary, the prediction about Israel's religious fall and current stubbornness demonstrates *her* fault. Additionally, Paul is preparing for the argumentation in chapter 10. He repeats the passage "whoever believes in him will not be put to shame" (Isa. 28:16) again in v. 11 (see below). As a whole, 9:30–33 prepare for the next argumentation in 10:1–3, as is seen in the following similarities:

- Pursuing νόμον δικαιοσύνης ("the law of righteousness" in 9:31) designates ζῆλος (a "zeal" for God, 10:2).
- The phrase ὡς ἐξ ἔργων ("as if it were based on works" in 9:32) denotes establishing "their own righteousness" (10:3).
- To stumble on ὁ λίθος τοῦ προσκόμματος ("the stumbling stone" in 9:32)—namely, on Christ (9:33)—coincides with not submitting to "God's righteousness" (10:3), or Christ (10:4), who in his own person is and has brought about righteousness (10:5ff.).[105]

Paul's argumentation culminates in v. 4, where he puts forth a thesis explaining his view of the relationship between the law and gospel:

Τέλος γὰρ νόμου χριστὸς εἰς δικαιοσύνην παντὶ τῷ πιστεύοντι.

For Christ is the end of the law for righteousness to everyone who believes.

The Greek word τέλος can designate either "end" or "goal" (other connotations that it may at times have are not discussed here). The latter *teleological* meaning often appears in ancient secular literature, whereas the former *temporal* meaning mainly occurs in the Septuagint and in the New Testament.[106] There is hardly a sharp contrast between the two nuances in v. 4. Rather, they complement each other at least to some degree.[107]

Yet given the argumentation in Romans, it seems best to translate the Greek text ("Christ is the end of the law") as the ESV and others do, even if the other aspect ("Christ is the goal of the law") should likewise be remembered. The following weighty reasons speak strongly for the first alternative:[108]

    a. The most common meaning of the word τέλος in the Septuagint and the New Testament is "end."[109]

    b. The context clearly pits the Mosaic Law and Christ against each other (see 9:31–33, 10:5ff.). The latter excludes the previous.[110]

    c. It is always "the law and the prophets" (all of the Old Testament) that witness Christ but not the law as such (see 3:21, which differentiates between "the law" and "the Law and the Prophets").[111]

    d. Christ would be the goal (or fulfillment) of the law even without faith. Still, v. 4 emphasizes that he is "the end of the law for righteousness [read: *only*] to everyone who believes."[112]

    e. Christ is the subject in v. 4. It is first and foremost a statement that refers to *his* relationship to the law. Thus

"Christ is the end of the law." Paul would have used the article τό before τέλος if he had intended that word to be the subject. In Greek, the word order is reversed for the sake of emphasis (cf., e.g., Phil. 2:11; 1 Thess. 4:6).[113] Provided that one interprets τέλος as "goal" or "fulfillment," the sentence rather tells of the *law's* relationship to Christ: "The goal/fulfillment of the law is Christ." To be sure, the difference is not monumental but also not insignificant.[114]

It is also important to take notice of the parallel structure between 3:20–22 and 10:3–4:

- The law cannot declare anyone righteous before God (3:20), and the Jews cannot establish their own righteousness (10:3).
- God's righteousness (or righteousness from God) has been revealed apart from the law (3:21), and Christ is the end of the law (10:4a).[115]
- God's righteousness is for everyone who believes (both 3:22 and 10:4b).[116]

Even the phrase in 3:21 "a righteousness μαρτυρουμένη ὑπὸ τοῦ νόμου καὶ τῶν προφητῶν" (which the Law and the Prophets bear witness to) corresponds to the argumentation from Scripture in chapter 10, where first a reference to the law (vv. 6–8) and then a few quotations from the prophets (vv. 11ff.) prevail.[117]

To sum up the previous discussion, Christ is the end of the law by being its final goal (cf. both aspects of the Greek word τέλος above). He fulfills the whole law with the purpose of dispensing with it in connection to righteousness.[118] Thus the investigation in 9:30–10:3 culminates in v. 4, which leads into the next section. The thesis regarding the relationship between the Torah and the Messiah is central for the discussion in 10:5–13 (see below).[119]

Verses 5–13 give the motivation for v. 4 (see the little particle "for") by accounting for how one may establish righteousness, which the Jews pursued but could not attain (9:31–32): first a *negative*

Scripture argument (v. 5) and then a *positive* argument (vv. 6–8) followed by further discussion (vv. 9–13).[120] Here, the Reformation's distinction between "law" and "gospel" especially stands out.[121]

The quotation in v. 5 begins with the phrase Μωϋσῆς γράφει ("Moses writes"). It is unusual that the verb is in the present tense here when otherwise it is found in perfect (γέγραπται). No other Old Testament passage is rendered in a similar way in the Pauline Epistles (an anomaly that will be examined more closely in connection with v. 6).[122] Verse 5 concerns "the righteousness that is based on the law":

Ὁ ποιήσας [αὐτὰ] ἄνθρωπος ζήσεται ἐν αὐτῇ [αὐτοῖς].

"The person who does the commandments shall live by them." (Lev. 18:5)

LXX: (ποιήσετε αὐτά,) ἃ ποιήσας ἄνθρωπος ζήσεται ἐν αὐτοῖς.

The quotation must first and foremost be interpreted against the backdrop of v. 3. There the focus lies on "righteousness from *God*" (God's righteousness). Here, on the contrary, the concern is the righteousness that *man* should reach by his own effort. Salvation depends to a high degree, if not completely, on his ability. The contrast between the two is obvious.[123]

From the beginning to the end, chapter 18 of Leviticus treats many "unlawful sexual relations." Israel is warned that the land will "vomit [them] out" if they are found guilty of such gross sins (v. 28). Therefore, the promise to "live" (v. 5) originally meant an assurance to live in the Promised Land. Yet a spiritual perspective was easily combined with it, and "life" was explained to refer primarily to eternal life in heaven. Paul seems to understand the text this way as well. Similarly, he understands the promise to Abraham to "be heir of the world" in Rom. 4:13 in equal terms (cf. Gen. 12:2–3, 13:15–17).[124]

Lev. 18 does not actually allow for any means of atonement for the sins enumerated in vv. 6–23. Exile is the only punishment prescribed for them (see especially vv. 24–30; cf. also 26:31–33).[125] Furthermore, it is of great interest that Lev. 18 is quoted many times already in the Old Testament to confirm the fair *judgment* over Israel as a result of their religious decay (see Neh. 9:29; Ezek. 20:11, 20:13, 20:21).[126] All this works well with the intention of the apostle. In his critique of justification by works, he overlooks various Jewish means of atonement. One who wants to win righteousness of the law has to attain complete fulfillment of the law. Anything less is insufficient (see the argumentation in Romans on the whole and especially Gal. 3:10, 5:3).[127] In addition, the development of salvation history in Scripture definitely shows that (eternal) life cannot be connected to any human merits. They always and only lead to judgment and (eternal) condemnation—in unison with a similar conclusion in Romans (see, e.g., chapters 1–3).[128]

Paul deliberately begins the new quotation in vv. 6–8 differently than in v. 5. Instead of the rare phrase γράφει ("writes"), he now uses λέγει ("says"). His language probably points to the distinct difference between the killing *letter* of the Mosaic Law and the living *voice* of the gospel (cf. 2:27–29, 7:6; 2 Cor. 3:6). Verse 5 relates to the former, vv. 6–8 to the latter.[129]

Actually, the one who speaks in vv. 6–8 surprisingly turns out to be ἡ ἐκ πίστεως δικαιοσύνη ("the righteousness by faith"). Paul again personifies his salvation terminology. He seems to identify it with Christ himself (cf. the Christological interpretation in vv. 6–8; see also above). Incidentally, a similar connection is made in Gal. 3:23–25 as well, where the faith that comes and the Christ who comes are synonymous expressions.[130]

The first sentence in the quotation "do not say in your heart" originates from Deut. 9:4. The verse and its context speak strongly against the self-righteousness of the Israelites:

> Do not say in your heart, after the LORD your God has thrust them out before you, "It is because of my righteousness that the LORD has brought me in to possess this land," whereas it is because of the wickedness of these nations that the LORD is driving them out before you. (see also vv. 5–6; cf., e.g., 8:17)

To begin with, Paul draws on that kind of thought and then moves on to his Christological application. He has the same intent as Deuteronomy (see below). Indeed, his whole argumentation in 9:30–10:3 has the same intent (see above). In addition, it should be taken into account that the term *heart* is found in the Old Testament quotation, which will become relevant in chapter 10 (see vv. 8–11, 14, 16–17).[131]

The second quotation in vv. 6–8 is from Deuteronomy as well (30:12–14). The text, together with some Pauline explanations, reads:

> Μὴ εἴπῃς ἐν τῇ καρδίᾳ σου Τίς ἀναβήσεται εἰς τὸν οὐρανόν; τοῦτ' ἔστιν Χριστὸν καταγαγεῖν·
>
> ἢ Τίς καταβήσεται εἰς τὴν ἄβυσσον; τοῦτ' ἔστιν Χριστὸν ἐκ νεκρῶν ἀναγαγεῖν.
>
> ἀλλὰ τί λέγει; Ἐγγύς σου τὸ ῥῆμά ἐστιν, ἐν τῷ στόματί σου καὶ ἐν τῇ καρδίᾳ σου· τοῦτ' ἔστιν τὸ ῥῆμα τῆς πίστεως ὃ κηρύσσομεν.

> "Who will ascend into heaven?" (that is, to bring Christ down).
>
> or "Who will descend into the abyss?" (that is, to bring Christ up from the dead).
>
> But what does it say? "The word is near you, in your mouth and in your heart" (that is, the word of faith that we proclaim). (vv. 6b–8)

Interpretation of this text has proven to be problematic. The question is whether Paul is quoting the Old Testament at all or only using its language for his own purposes.[132] Although he adds short explanations "between the lines," the text itself obviously has to be understood as his quotation from Scripture. In Romans, the verb "say" (v. 6) often introduces a scriptural passage (see, e.g., 9:15, 9:17, 9:25, 10:11, 10:16, 10:19, 10:20, 10:21, 11:2, 11:4, 11:9). Moreover, the contrast between v. 5 and vv. 6–8 presupposes that an Old Testament quotation stands out in both cases.[133]

A much more comprehensive problem concerns the understanding of Scripture that Paul reads into his text. Is his Christological application an arbitrary distortion of the original meaning? Or is there perhaps an underlying cause to his line of thought? Indeed, it does not make it easier to deal with the problem on account of the fact that Lev. 18:5 and Deut. 30:12–14, different parts of the *same* Torah, are put in sharp contrast to each other in vv. 5–8. Do we face a deadlock that is not to be broken here? For this reason, it is absolutely necessary to take a closer look at the theological perspective in Deuteronomy.[134]

In his farewell speech in Deuteronomy, Moses harshly reproaches the Israelites for their disobedience and stubbornness. He stresses to them, "To this day the LORD has not given you a heart to understand or eyes to see or ears to hear" (29:4). The people in general, with only a few exceptions, have been stiff-necked during the journey in the wilderness and will continue the same lifestyle in the future as well (see 31:27–29). Therefore, God has definitely not chosen Israel based on her merits. Behind his election lies only grace and love for them (9:4–6, which is alluded to in Rom. 10:6a). Moreover, to say the obvious already beforehand: the Israelites will be driven out of their country. At long last, they have to bear the curse that falls on them (28:15ff., 31:16–18). Yet in the Lord's vision of the future, there is the promise that he will finally end their exile and circumcise their hearts. A new and bright future will begin for his chosen people (30:1–10).[135] Hence Deut. 30:11–14 (or vv. 12–14 as quoted in Rom. 10:6–8) is framed by such an eschatological context. Against that kind of background, the Israelites are apparently not able to keep the commandments. The Mosaic exhortations do not have much effect on them.

Likewise, in Romans, Paul reproaches the Jews of his time in general for having uncircumcised hearts (2:28–29). His view of them and the whole of mankind culminates in the insight of a deep corruption (3:9–18). He explicitly refers to Lev. 18:5, which is related to the curse of the law especially in the prophetic proclamation (10:5; see above). Promptly thereafter, he introduces his proof from Deut. 30:12–14 with a short phrase from Deut. 9:4, which in its context renounces human self-righteousness (10:6a; see above). The Christological application of the scriptural exhortation to keep the law (10:6b–8) means, under such circumstances, that Christ has done what no one else has been able to. He has truly kept all the Old Testament commands—he alone! Since the Israelites fell short in their attempt to keep the law, Deut. 30:12–14 has never become a reality in their own lives but is in the deepest sense fulfilled first in Christ. He has accomplished everything that is written.[136]

Accordingly, 10:6–8 gives a concrete example of how Christ is the end of the law by fulfilling it (see v. 4 above). He has earned salvation for everyone who believes. The contrast between righteousness by the law and righteousness by faith simply coincides with the principal question of who should and is able to keep the law. There are two entirely opposite answers: either the Jew and man in general or Christ himself. The different responses lead to two differing ways of reading the Old Testament. The inventive reorientation in the Pauline exposition of Scripture bears heavily upon the spiritual and, at the same time, literal meaning of the texts. Without a doubt, they markedly testify about Christ, but he only appears to the eyes of faith.

What then has Christ done to win that righteousness toward which Deut. 30:12–14 points? The apostolic exposition in Rom. 10 speaks about his incarnation and resurrection (vv. 6–7). The phrase "ascend into heaven" (v. 6) corresponds to the idea of "bringing Christ down," figurative language that depicts something impossible. It implies that he became man (the beginning of his work of salvation).[137] The other phrase to "descend into the abyss" (v. 7) corresponds to the idea of "bringing Christ up from the dead," figurative language that depicts something equally impossible. Here the word of the original text "sea" (Deut. 30:13) is substituted with "abyss." They are occasionally identical terms (see, e.g., Jon. 2:3–10; cf. Targum Neofiti), but the latter evidently fits the spiritual application better. Christ is risen from his grave (the end of his work of salvation).[138] As a result, the temporal frames for the preparation of righteousness by faith have been precisely defined. They extend from the holy moment of conception to the exuberant joy of Easter morning. Everything that Christ did during that period constitutes the foundation for salvation. Or expressed in dogmatic terms, both his active and passive obedience are part of the atonement at Golgotha.

The righteousness that Christ earned is passed on through the word (= the gospel), which "is near you, in your mouth and in your heart" (v. 8), a statement that recalls Isaiah's proclamation with regard to the "righteousness that draws near" (e.g., 46:13, 51:5, 56:1).[139] With such a prophetic background, it is easy to understand why Paul explicitly combines his quotation from Deuteronomy with righteousness by faith. Consequently, he further adds as an explanation: "That is, the word of faith that we proclaim" (v. 8). There has been a long discussion about whether the addition suggests "the content of faith" (*fides quae creditur*) or "the act of believing" (*fides qua creditur*). Maybe both alternatives are partially right: the phrase "the word of faith" surely stands for the gospel (*fides quae creditur*) that works faith (*fides qua creditur*). It is a "both/and," not an exclusive "either/or" (cf. the next verses with the same intention).[140]

As mentioned earlier, v. 8 (Deut. 30:14) introduces the pair of phrases "in your mouth" and "in your heart," which constitutes the constant theme in chapter 10 according to the following outline:

- the mouth (and the confession of the mouth) in vv. 9–10, 12–14 (to "call" on the name of the Lord) and
- the heart (and the faith of the heart) in vv. 9–11, 14, 16–17.

The quotation in v. 21 also alludes to the same pair of phrases:

- ἀπειθοῦντα ("disobedient") = one who is not convinced of the gospel in his heart
- ἀντιλέγοντα ("contrary") = one who speaks contrary to the gospel[141]

The argumentation that follows in chapter 10 is influenced by the word order in Deut. 30:14. Verse 9 repeats the dichotomy "mouth—heart" in this order. After that, v. 10 continues the reasoning in reversed order "heart—mouth" (a chiastic structure A–B–B–A). Then the reading in v. 11 makes the connection to "the heart" and the reading in vv. 12–13 to "the mouth." The clarity of the composition is impressive. Next, the message as a Christological interpretation of the prophetic word from the perspective of the gospel will be examined.[142]

Verse 9 gives a short summary of the phrase "the word of faith that we proclaim" in v. 8. To begin with, the early church's first creed, "Jesus is Lord," is repeated. Then the foundational conviction that "God raised him from the dead" is reiterated. Both doctrinal beliefs are obviously connected to the Christian rite of baptism. The latter presupposes the prior. Jesus' resurrection proves that he is the Lord—that is, the Lord who has revealed himself in the Old Testament, in harmony with the Christological exposition of Scripture in vv. 6–8 (see also 9:5–6 above).[143] Indeed, to believe in him and confess him means that the word is "near": in the heart

and the mouth. Already here and especially later in v. 10, it is clear
that the argumentation refers back to the theme verses of Romans
(1:16–17; see above):

Καρδίᾳ γὰρ πιστεύεται εἰς δικαιοσύνην, στόματι δὲ ὁμολογεῖται εἰς
σωτηρίαν.

For with the heart one believes and is justified, and with the mouth
one confesses and is saved. (v. 10)

The language and content (faith, righteousness, salvation) are
similar in both chapter 1 and chapter 10. They revolve around the
conditions for entrance to eternal life.[144]

Moreover, v. 11 provides motivation for the preceding with a
quotation, just as 1:16–17, which ends with Hab. 2:4. Here, the same
portion of Isa. 28:16 as already quoted in 9:33 is repeated:

Πᾶς ὁ πιστεύων ἐπ᾽ αὐτῷ οὐ καταισχυνθήσεται.

"Everyone who believes in him will not be put to shame."

LXX: Ὁ πιστεύων ἐπ᾽ αὐτῷ οὐ μὴ καταισχυνθῇ.

Paul adds the word πᾶς ("everyone") in agreement with his own
emphasis in v. 4 ("to everyone who believes").[145] He has now come
one step further in his argumentation. To "be put to shame" should
primarily not be interpreted psychologically but rather with the last
day in mind. The phrase alludes to the condemned who shame themselves at the final judgment (cf. 5:5).[146] They will be excluded from the
heavenly kingdom. In other words, the Old Testament quotation (Isa.
28:16) in v. 10 is characterized by a strong eschatological perspective, a feature that is also true of the Old Testament quotation (Hab.
2:4) in 1:17. Besides, 1:16 speaks, in a similar way, about "not [being]
ashamed of the gospel," which will give salvation on the last day.[147]

Verse 12 explains more closely the promise in Isa. 28:16. The
Greek word πᾶς is found here as well. There is no difference between

Jews and Gentiles, "for the same Lord is Lord of all, bestowing his riches on all who call on him" (cf. 3:22–23, 3:29–30).[148]

The next scriptural reference in v. 13, from Joel 2:32, again repeats the word πᾶς and also the previous verb "call on."[149]

Πᾶς γὰρ ὃς ἂν ἐπικαλέσηται τὸ ὄνομα Κυρίου σωθήσεται.

For "everyone who calls on the name of the LORD shall be saved."

LXX: Πᾶς, ὃς ἂν ἐπικαλέσηται τὸ ὄνομα κυρίου, σωθήσεται·

On the whole, the context of the verse has several connections to the apostolic message:

a. The Lord is Christ (see above).
b. Joel 2:28–29 talks about the pouring out of the Spirit, which in the New Covenant is realized by faith.
c. Joel 2:28 prophesies that the Spirit will be poured "on all flesh," even on the Gentiles, in concert with Rom. 10:11–12.
d. Joel 2:26–27 predicts (twice) that in the future the Lord's people will never "be put to shame," a view that connects to Isa. 28:16 and Rom. 10:11.
e. Joel 2:32 on the one hand emphasizes that "everyone who calls on the name of the LORD shall be saved" but on the other hand stresses no one else but those "delivered" or a "remnant" in Israel will be saved—as Rom. 9:27 (see further vv. 6–13, 29; cf. 11:1–10) stresses in connection to Isa. 10:22.

According to old established Jewish custom, one should each time (if necessary) also read the context of the quotation, which apparently has been done here.[150]

Through repetition of the verb ἐπικαλεῖσθαι ("to call upon"), vv. 13 and 14 are associated with each other.[151] In vv. 14–15, there are, in total, four rhetorical questions beginning with the interrogative "how" that in depth explain Joel 2:32. The thought goes "backward": from the confession of the mouth, to the faith of the heart, to hearing, and finally to proclamation as well as sending. It seems as if the verses leading up to v. 18 speak of man in general, but at least of the Jews in particular (cf. vv. 19–21).[152] Verse 15 speaks about the proclaimers of the gospel and applies Isa. 52:7 to their mission work (cf. Nah. 1:15 as a parallel passage):

Ὡς ὡραῖοι οἱ πόδες τῶν εὐαγγελιζομένων ἀγαθά.

"How beautiful are the feet of those who preach the good news!"

LXX: Ὡς ὥρα ἐπὶ τῶν ὀρέων, ὡς πόδες εὐαγγελιζομένου ἀκοὴν εἰρήνης, ὡς εὐαγγελιζόμενος ἀγαθά.

Instead of the singular like in the Septuagint, the plural is used here ("messengers of joy"), with regard to all apostles and preachers.[153] Their footsteps are beautiful because they bring the gospel concerning forgiveness of sins. The word ὡραῖοι could also mean that they come "at the right time," a phrase that mainly refers to the gospel as the most crucial eschatological turning point in salvation history. Obviously, Paul has the Jews in mind specifically since he already in 2:24 quotes Isa. 52:5 with application to them.[154] Additionally, chapters 9–11 as a whole consider their unbelief. Verses 14–15 argue that God in fact has sent out his messengers and that he, through their proclamation, calls his chosen people and other people to repentance.[155]

The universal address of the gospel (vv. 9–13) does not, however, correspond to the hard reality of this world. Certainly, everyone who calls upon the name of the Lord will be saved (v. 13), but according to v. 16, "not all" want to trust him (litotes, a rhetorical device that denies the opposite and in actual fact implies that "most" do not want; cf. the idea of a remnant in 9:6, 9:27).[156] They are not willing to obey the gospel, as the prophet Isaiah (53:1) predicts:

Κύριε, τίς ἐπίστευσεν τῇ ἀκοῇ ἡμῶν;

"Lord, who has believed what he has heard from us?"

The quotation follows LXX verbatim without any changes.

"[To not] obey the gospel" (οὐ ὑπήκουσαν τῷ εὐαγγελίῳ) and "[to not] believe our message" (τίς ἐπίστευσεν τῇ ἀκοῇ ἡμῶν;) in v. 16 are synonymous in their content (see, e.g., 1:5, 16:26, where "obedience" and "faith" are connected to each other). Linguistically, ὑπακοή ("obedience") suggests that one, so to say, stands ὑπό ("under") ἀκοή ("the preaching").[157] In light of Jewish tradition, Isa. 53:1 more closely relates to the apostolic proclamation. The Targum translates the Hebrew word שְׁמוּעָה with the Aramaic word בְּשׂוֹרָה, "message of joy." If it were possible for such a translation to have been in use prior to the destruction of Jerusalem in AD 70, then an obvious parallel to the Christian message of joy, the gospel, is found here.[158]

Verse 17 draws a conclusion from the previous verses.[159] Even if not all believe the Christian proclamation, faith still "comes from hearing, and hearing through the word of Christ" (ἡ πίστις ἐξ ἀκοῆς, ἡ δὲ ἀκοὴ διὰ ῥήματος Χριστοῦ). Indeed, there are no other ways for faith to be created. Besides, the same Greek word ἀκοή denotes either "that which is heard" or "hearing." Therefore, both of the following translations are valid:

    a. Thus faith comes by preaching and preaching by the word of Christ (see v. 16).
    b. Thus faith comes by hearing and hearing by the word of Christ (see vv. 14, 18, where the corresponding word *hear* occurs; cf. further Gal. 3:2).[160]

In Greek, the two alternatives merge. "That which is heard" assumes "hearing" as well as "hearing" assumes "that which is heard." Both have their origin in "Christ's word." Precisely, the phrase does not refer to the Christian message of him per se but rather to the gospel as a fulfillment of the Old Testament promises in him. Verse 8 speaks of τὸ ῥῆμα τῆς πίστεως ("the word of faith") in a similar way and combines it with a Christological reading of the Old Testament (see vv. 6–8).[161] It is exactly such a view of the

Bible that, according to v. 17, creates faith (cf. the conversion of the disciples in Luke 24:25–27, 24:44–48), a truth that deserves to be given serious attention, not the least in churchly circles.[162]

If faith has its origin in hearing (v. 17), then it naturally follows whether one has heard the gospel (v. 18) and also whether one has understood it (v. 19). The pronoun *they* in v. 18 obviously refers to the Israelites in v. 19. Paul explicitly focuses on their relationship to the apostolic proclamation (see above). In light of Ps. 19:5, he argues that they certainly have heard:

Εἰς πᾶσαν τὴν γῆν ἐξῆλθεν ὁ φθόγγος αὐτῶν, καὶ εἰς τὰ πέρατα τῆς οἰκουμένης τὰ ῥήματα αὐτῶν.

"Their voice has gone out to all the earth, and their words to the ends of the world."

The quotation follows LXX (Ps. 18:5) verbatim without any changes.

Ps. 19:4 actually speaks about *general* revelation ("their voice" alludes to the witness of the heavens as to the creation). Later in vv. 8–12, the notion is associated with the *special* revelation (the teaching in the Torah). According to Jewish reasoning, there is hardly any definite difference between the two. The Lord's speaking always permeates the whole universe. If one rejects his law, one violates his absolute order of creation. Therefore, general revelation leads—without saying—to special revelation.[163]

Against the background of Ps. 19 as a whole, it is easy to see that Paul applies v. 5 to the apostolic proclamation. He takes for granted that the gospel reinforces and confirms the original message of creation. By faith, man becomes "a new creation" (2 Cor. 5:17) "created after the likeness of God" (Eph. 4:24) or "after the image of its Creator" (Col. 3:10). He gets his true humanity back, which was lost due to the fall. Here in Romans, the whole argumentation is built on Hebrew thinking.[164]

Still, the challenge remains how Paul dares at all to claim that the gospel has "gone out to all the earth" already in his day. There are a number of attempts to explain his bold thesis. Some of the most important are presented as follows:

a. Paul exaggerates (hyperbole).[165]
b. Paul talks about so-called corporative units, the Gentiles and Jews in general (but not every single individual).[166]
c. Paul understands the Greek word οἰκουμένη as a designation of the Roman Empire (but not the whole universe).[167]

It might turn out that each alternative deserves both attention and reflection. Yet the undeniable fact is that here Paul focuses mainly on the mission to the Jews (vv. 19–21; see the argumentation on the whole in chapters 9–11). In line with his multiple years of experience, *they* all over the world have heard something about himself and the gospel (cf., e.g., Acts 17:6, 21:28, 24:5, 28:22). From that perspective, v. 18 hardly seems exaggerated.[168]

Verse 18 can, for the sake of clarity, be translated and paraphrased as follows:

> Their voice (i.e., "the gospel") has gone out (or ingressive aorist: "began to go out") to (εἰς: "into") all the earth and their words to (εἰς: "into") the end of the world.

In addition, it cannot be ruled out that Paul's entire mission strategy culminates in v. 18. Provided that he equates the gospel with the sun (cf. the religious expression: "the sun of grace"), which enlightens the whole world (see Ps. 19:5 in comparison with 2 Cor. 4:6), their "moving paths" correspond to each other. The sun "rises at one end of the heavens and makes its circuit to the other" (Ps. 19:6 NIV; cf. further v. 5). In the same way, the gospel has now begun its "circuit" from Jerusalem (= east) and will continue to Spain (= west) according to the plans in Rom. 15:17–29 (cf. Col. 1:23).[169]

In v. 19, Paul sets forth his argumentation in regard to the unbelief of the Israelites. Now he asks if after hearing the gospel they perhaps did not understand it. The question assumes that they have understood. The problem is not at all a lack of comprehension from their part. In contrast, they do grasp the gospel, but they do not embrace it. Put differently, they do not receive it in faith.[170] Hence

God's chosen people rejected God's word![171] This absurd situation is certainly not easy to explain, but Paul undertakes it with the help of Holy Scripture. He quotes a passage from Deuteronomy (32:21):

Ἐγὼ παραζηλώσω ὑμᾶς ἐπ' οὐκ ἔθνει, ἐπ' ἔθνει ἀσυνέτῳ παροργιῶ ὑμᾶς.

"I will make you jealous of those who are not a nation; with a foolish nation I will make you angry."

LXX: Κἀγὼ παραζηλώσω αὐτοὺς ἐπ' οὐκ ἔθνει, ἐπ' ἔθνει ἀσυνέτῳ παροργιῶ αὐτούς.

The quotation in content amounts to Hosea 2:23 as stated in Rom. 9:25 with the nearly identical statement about a "no nation" (see above). In its original context, Deut. 32:21 speaks of God's punishments for the idolatry of the Israelites. He will soon repay them according to their iniquities. The retaliation will come in the form of a foreign people devastating their whole country.[172] Paul interprets the verse typologically and applies it to the calling of the Gentiles through the gospel. He argues that the rejection of the Messiah in reality coincides with the former idolatry, a detail reminiscent of the argumentation in 9:1–5 (Christ is Israel's God; see above) and 9:6–24 (where unbelieving Jews are equated with Ismael, Esau, Pharaoh, and "the vessels of wrath").[173] The direct address in second-person plural, instead of third-person plural as in Deut. 32:21, further emphasizes Israel's guilt. They actually have a personal responsibility for their opposing stance.[174]

The jealousy and ferocity that the Israelites feel owing to Paul's law-free mission to the Gentiles show with certainty that they have fully heard and understood his gospel. Otherwise, their reaction against him would be entirely inconceivable. For that reason, he quotes Deut. 32:21 as his first evidence for the comprehension of the Israelites. His second evidence for their adverse attitude he finds in Isa. 65:1–2. Yet another passage from the Torah (see further above 9:12–13) gets its exposition by prophetic text according to the Jewish way of arguing.[175] In v. 20, Paul has the same intention as in v. 19.

He quotes Isa. 65:1 to emphasize the admission of the Gentiles into Israel, which will make God's chosen people "jealous of those who are not a nation" (v. 19):

Εὑρέθην τοῖς ἐμὲ μὴ ζητοῦσιν, ἐμφανὴς ἐγενόμην τοῖς ἐμὲ μὴ ἐπερωτῶσιν.

"I have been found by those who did not seek me; I have shown myself to those who did not ask for me."

LXX (the order of the phrases is reversed with minor changes): Ἐμφανὴς ἐγενόμην τοῖς ἐμὲ μὴ ζητοῦσιν, εὑρέθην τοῖς ἐμὲ μὴ ἐπερωτῶσιν·

Isa. 65:2, on the other hand, is directed toward Israel and is quoted in v. 21:

Ὅλην τὴν ἡμέραν ἐξεπέτασα τὰς χεῖράς μου πρὸς λαὸν ἀπειθοῦντα καὶ ἀντιλέγοντα.

"All day long I have held out my hands to a disobedient and contrary people."

LXX: Ἐξεπέτασα τὰς χεῖράς μου ὅλην τὴν ἡμέραν πρὸς λαὸν ἀπει-θοῦντα καὶ ἀντιλέγοντα.

There has been much discussion as to whether Isa. 65:1–2 as a whole pertains only to Israel. But at least according to the Septuagint, v. 1 for sure relates to "the Gentiles" (ἔθνος) and v. 2 to "the Jews" (λαός). The corresponding words in Hebrew are גוֹי (v. 1) and עַם (v. 2). Although the language varies, the former seems, in light of Isa. 42:1, 42:6, and 49:6, really to refer to the Gentiles and the latter to the Jews (further see, e.g., Gen. 22:18, 26:4).[176] Moreover, it is not certain how the rest of Isa. 65:1 should be translated. There are two distinguished alternatives: "to a people who did not call on my name" and "to a people who was not named after my name." The former rather alludes to Israel, who in their religious apostasy do not trust in the Lord. The latter alludes to the Gentiles, who in their appalling wickedness do not belong to the Lord. According to the Masoretic vocalization, the verb קֹרָא should be interpreted as passive (*pual*) of קָרָא. In that case, the text has to be translated in agreement with the second alternative: "to a people who was not named after my name."[177] Yet it is not wholly excluded that the Gentiles are included even in the first alternative: "to a people who did not call on my name" (cf. LXX).[178]

The quotation from Isa. 65:1–2 concludes the discussion in the entire section of 9:30–10:21. At the same time, it points back to the beginning (*inclusio*). The Gentiles who did not seek God but found him (10:20) are precisely those who did not pursue righteousness but attained it (9:30). In contrast, Israel is a disobedient and obstinate people (10:21), which causes her to reject her Messiah and stumble on the stumbling stone (9:31–33). With such parallels, the main content of the passage is repeated as well as the extended argumentation summarized insightfully.[179]

After Israel's faults have been brought to light, a question still remains: has God definitely abandoned his people because of their apostasy? Is there no place for them in his plan of salvation? In view of that, the discussion has to continue in chapter 11, where the edge of the veil of the future is lifted.

(5) 11:1–10

Paul begins chapter 11 with a question that closely and easily connects it to the last verse in chapter 10. He asks if God has allegedly "rejected his people." The verb ἀπώθειν has a very concrete meaning. It literally means "to repel" with his hands. Since God has held out his hands all day long to a rebellious and obstinate people (10:21), the question—as expected—arises as to whether he has held out his hands only to repel his people.[180] No, that is not possible. "By no means" (μὴ γένοιτο)![181] Paul uses himself as an example of a Jew who has not been rejected (v. 1).[182] Then he adds, as further assertion, the general sentence that God has not rejected his people (v. 2).[183] This functions as the great theme for vv. 1–32. Verses 1–10 stand as a link between Israel's past/present time (9:6–10:21) and future

(11:11–32). Paul talks about the remnant primarily with a negative purpose especially in 9:27–29: *only* a remnant will be saved. Yet in 11:1–10, he talks about the remnant with a positive purpose: there still *is* a remnant that will be saved.[184]

In fact, v. 2a reproduces both 1 Sam. 12:22 and Ps. 94:14, which according to the Septuagint (see also Biblia Hebraica) have the exact same word order:

Οὐκ ἀπώσατο ὁ θεὸς τὸν λαὸν αὐτοῦ.

"God has not rejected his people."

LXX: Οὐκ ἀπώσεται κύριος τὸν λαὸν αὐτοῦ.[185]

This promise regarding the Lord's protection and support in the future prevails for Israel despite the fact that they do not deserve it in the slightest. Quite the opposite, they have abandoned him as their King (1 Sam. 12). Moreover, they suffer agony and torment under enemies because of their gross sins (Ps. 94). Even if it is difficult to understand precisely what Paul intends with his quotation, the Old Testament context fits well with the historical situation during his time: Israel has abandoned her King, the Messiah, and lives under the tyranny of Rome. The future of the people is threatened by a total catastrophe (cf. the development during AD 66–70).[186] Nevertheless, God's promise stands firm. He does not want to reject his people. The conviction is based on God's gracious choice. He "foreknew" (προέγνω) Israel as his own. The verb *foreknow* assumes the election of the people (cf. Amos 3:2a), which embraces not only a small remnant but *all* of Israel.[187] They still have, even in their unbelief, a special position among the other people in the world (see vv. 28–29; cf. 9:1–5 above).[188] After the thorough argumentation in 9:30–10:21, such a conclusion seems a little surprising but nevertheless worthy of attention.

Verse 2b then draws on the story of Elijah's fight against Baal's prophets (a combination of LXX 1 Kings 19:10 and 19:14).[189] In his anguish and anxiety, he turns to God with the following prayer:

Κύριε, τοὺς προφήτας σου ἀπέκτειναν, τὰ θυσιαστήριά σου κατέσκα-
ψαν, κἀγὼ ὑπελείφθην μόνος καὶ ζητοῦσιν τὴν ψυχήν μου.

"Lord, they have killed your prophets, they have demolished your
altars, and I alone am left, and they seek my life." (v. 3)

Though the clauses are reproduced in a slightly different order, the
quotation is undeniably from 1 Kings 19:10 and 19:14 without any
meaningful changes.[190]

Immediately thereafter, God's response is quoted:

Κατέλιπον ἐμαυτῷ ἑπτακισχιλίους ἄνδρας, οἵτινες οὐκ ἔκαμψαν
γόνυ τῇ Βάαλ.

"I have kept for myself seven thousand men who have not bowed the
knee to Baal." (v. 4)

The text is from 1 Kings 19:18 with a few insignificant changes.[191]

The application of the two quotations follows in v. 5. It is once
again based on a typological exposition (see already 9:6ff.). As in
Elijah's time, there was in Paul's time, and even still, a remnant who
believe in the Lord and will be saved.[192] Consequently, "unbelief in
gospel" is almost identical with Baal's worship—a very heightened
conclusion like the previous comparisons between Isaac and Ismael
or Jacob and Esau (9:6–13), the narrative about Pharaoh's hardened
heart (9:14–18), the parable about "the vessels of wrath" (9:20–24),
and the accusation of idolatry (10:19).[193]

Since 1 Kings 19:18 explicitly underscores that God in his
mercy has reserved for himself faithful men, his actions are based
on nothing but grace and not on human merits. Verses 5–6 emphasize that point of view. Here, our works do not count. They are completely excluded, "otherwise grace would no longer be grace" (v. 6).
Then v. 7 relates the doctrine of predestination (for the talk about the
chosen and becoming hardened, see 9:6–29) to the notion of man's
full responsibility (for the talk about "pursuing" and "reaching,"
see 9:30–10:21). The Israelites in general have not reached what
they have been pursuing with zeal. Only the elect have attained

righteousness; the others are hardened (cf. 9:30–31). Yet both groups belong to Israel, here as well as in v. 2 (cf. 9:6–7). The special status of the people does not change even for the sake of nonbelief, although in that case, they certainly lose their part in the coming kingdom.[194]

Deep down, God is behind the hardening in v. 7. His work is expressed, according to the Jewish manner, with the help of so-called divine passive (ἐπωρώθησαν, *passivum divinum*). Next, vv. 8–10 explain the assertion with a number of texts, which draw on the three parts of the Old Testament: the Torah (Deut. 29:4), the Prophets (Isa. 29:10), and the Writings (Ps. 69:23–24).[195] Verse 8 principally quotes Deut. 29:4 but adds "a spirit of stupor" from Isa. 29:10 (instead of "a heart to understand")[196] and accordingly changes—together with a few small variations—the negative clause ("the Lord has *not* given") to a positive clause ("God has given") in support of the direct act of hardening on God's part in v. 7b.[197] Thus the quotation now goes:

Ἔδωκεν αὐτοῖς ὁ Θεὸς πνεῦμα κατανύξεως, ὀφθαλμοὺς τοῦ μὴ βλέπειν καὶ ὦτα τοῦ μὴ ἀκούειν, ἕως τῆς σήμερον ἡμέρας.

"God gave them a spirit of stupor, eyes that would not see and ears that would not hear, down to this very day."

Then vv. 9–10 quote Ps. 69:23–24 with a few minor changes:[198]

Γενηθήτω ἡ τράπεζα αὐτῶν εἰς παγίδα καὶ εἰς θήραν καὶ εἰς σκάνδαλον καὶ εἰς ἀνταπόδομα αὐτοῖς,
     σκοτισθήτωσαν οἱ ὀφθαλμοὶ αὐτῶν τοῦ μὴ βλέπειν, καὶ τὸν νῶτον αὐτῶν διὰ παντὸς σύνκαμψον.

"Let their table become a snare and a trap, a stumbling block and a retribution for them;
     let their eyes be darkened so that they cannot see, and bend their backs forever."

The whole argumentation in vv. 8–10 relates to "eyes that would not see" as the common subject.[199] All of that reminds of Isa. 6:9–10, a passage the New Testament often recurs to when explaining the spiritual hardening among the Jews (see, e.g., Mark 4:12 and its parallels in John 12:40; Acts 28:26–27).[200] Their obstinate unbelief in the gospel especially in v. 7 goes back to the obduracy, which according to the Old Testament witness has already happened to them numerous times and is repeated once again. Still, it has never been final. Hence there is hope for the future, which will be fulfilled in the eschatological turning point (11:26–27; see below).[201]

Occasionally the metaphorical language in vv. 9–10 has been analyzed down to the smallest detail. Who knows whether the "table" (v. 9) refers to the Jewish sacrificial cult[202] or the table fellowship of Pharisees?[203] Who says if "bent backs" (v. 10) portrays the Roman tyranny?[204] Perchance the whole argumentation from Scripture here depicts the time of the crucifixion of Jesus. The Passover Seder was celebrated, but he received vinegar for his thirst (see Ps. 69:22). Then the verses quoted in Rom. 11:9–10 (Ps. 69:23–24) follow. Does the Old Testament context result in a deeper interpretation by Paul? Does he imply that the happy celebration of Passover, without worrying about the suffering and death of Jesus, was a reason for the hardening of the Jews? At least the subsequent fall of Jerusalem was in fact caused by their blind trust in temple worship and their permanent rejection of the Messiah. In that case, their "table" has indeed become a "snare" and a "trap" for them.[205] For sure, there are no easy conclusions.

Anyway, the hardening of the Jews appears easier to comprehend from the overall perspective of the Gentile mission. After they first rejected the gospel, it spread widely, throughout the whole world (vv. 11–12).[206] A more thorough explanation is put forth in the next pericope.

(6) 11:11–32

The pericope begins in the same way as the previous one, with the phrase λέγω ("I ask"). A provocative question follows and a direct negative answer, amounting to a longer exposition.[207] Gradually, Paul goes from a strict argumentation from Scripture to practical measures pertaining to the relationship in the church between Jewish and Gentile Christians. For that reason, he largely avoids quoting the Old Testament, other than in vv. 26b–27. Needless to say, the whole presentation still overflows with Old Testament allusions, not the least because to some extent he builds on what he already has presented in chapters 9–10 (cf., e.g., the notion of "envy" in 10:19, 11:11, as well as the thought of "stumbling" in 9:33, 11:11).[208]

Starting in v. 11, Paul first and foremost explains the key events in salvation history. He argues that Israel's stubbornness, something negative in itself, has caused something positive. Through "their trespass salvation has come to the Gentiles," which in turn will make them "jealous" and long for the same deliverance (vv. 11–12).[209] Hence there is no reason for the Gentile Christians in Rome to be arrogant toward Jewish Christians or Jews in general. That kind of erroneous attitude affirms that one has misunderstood God's plan of salvation in history.[210] He has consigned all to disobedience so that he may have mercy on all (v. 32). In particular, the parable about the olive tree (vv. 16–24) addresses human boasting at large. It shows that the Gentile Christians do not exist independently from Israel's past history and traditions. On the contrary, Israel is the "root" that carries the Gentile Christians as "branches" (v. 18).[211] Maybe certain adversaries have even argued that Paul himself as a former Pharisee has now abandoned the mission to the Jews to work solely as the apostle of the Gentiles. Here, he wants to repudiate the false rumor and demonstrate his loyalty toward his countrymen and the Old Testament heritage (vv. 13–15).[212]

Because the line of thought in vv. 11–24 entails virtually no scriptural readings, the passage will not be addressed here. Instead we will move directly to vv. 11:25–27, which yet again takes up references to the Old Testament. Verses 28–32 are to be discussed inasmuch as they shed light on the interpretation.

Verse 25 reveals a mystery, which vv. 26–27 more in depth explain.[213] It says that πώρωσις ἀπὸ μέρους ("a hardening in part") has come upon (in Greek, γέγονεν expresses God's activity) Israel, but in the end, πᾶς Ἰσραήλ ("all Israel") will be saved as the heavenly Deliverer intervenes.[214] The prediction about salvation is mainly based on

    a. the testimony of Scripture (vv. 26b–27),

b. the faithfulness of God toward his covenant and promise (vv. 28–29), and

c. the observation that God acts in the same manner with all people as well as with the intention to show them his mercy (vv. 30–32) and be praised by them (vv. 33–36).[215]

The argumentation in chapters 9–11, or even in the whole letter, culminates in the revelation of the mystery (v. 25).[216] It is completely thinkable that Paul has received knowledge about Israel's national restoration in the future through *one* specific revelation by studying *the* specific revelation—that is, Holy Scripture (vv. 26b–27). In his thinking, the former does not exclude the latter. In addition, he warns against trusting in one's own wisdom (v. 25, the original Greek referring to Prov. 3:7). Considering all the Old Testament allusions and quotations in the chapters 9–11, it does not seem plausible that the climax itself in the presentation would lack a scriptural argument.[217]

The term πᾶς Ἰσραήλ ("all Israel" in v. 26) goes back to Old Testament language. It apparently refers to the *ethnic* Israel, which Paul also speaks about previously in v. 25b. For certain, he does not intend the *spiritual* Israel, the Christian church, which is made up of both Jews and Gentiles. Should the mystery in v. 25 ultimately stand for the simple truth that all Christians will be saved?[218] That kind of interpretation would only increase the arrogance of the Gentile Christians toward the Jewish Christians even more (cf. above). Moreover, the Christian church cannot be portrayed as currently "enemies" (v. 28) or now "disobedient" (v. 31).[219] In Old Testament language, "*all* Israel" never refers to "*every* Israelite" but includes the *nation* Israel as a whole, disregarding a few individuals who for one reason or another do not count (such as apostates).[220] Further, πᾶς Ἰσραήλ ("all Israel") as a term is in agreement with πλήρωμα ("the full number") of Israel in v. 12, which correspond to πλήρωμα ("the full number") of the Gentiles in v. 25. Just as not every single Gentile will be saved, likewise not every single Israelite will be.[221] Notwithstanding, a slight difference between diachronic and synchronic perspectives may be seen: even if all Israelites in all times (the diachronic alternative) without doubt do not inherit the coming kingdom, all Israel will at the end of all history (the synchronic alternative) attain eternal life (bearing in mind the previous reservations).[222]

The Pauline vision of all Israel's salvation in the future counteracts an anti-Semitic or anti-Jewish approach.[223] Besides, it is closely related to the theme in chapters 9–11, which mainly argues that God's word has not failed (9:6) and that he has not rejected his people (11:1). Thus the trustworthiness of the Old Testament writings is emphasized: "So let it be written, so let it be done."[224] Yet Israel's special status does not suggest that her coming salvation could be fulfilled in any other way than through faith in Jesus Christ. He alone saves (10:4–13; see above). There is only *one* olive tree (11:16–24).[225] Despite his real hope for the future, Paul seems to be aware of the fact that he himself will not mark a turning point in the mission action among the Israelites. He tries to "save *some* of them" (11:14).[226] Notwithstanding his best and most serious efforts, the end-time reversal or revival among them tarries.

Ultimately, a direct answer concerning questions of time is missing in chapter 11, but at least three clarifications are given:

a. ἡ πρόσλημψις (the "acceptance") of the Israelites means ζωὴ ἐκ νεκρῶν ("life from the dead" in v. 15).[227]
b. Their repentance will not happen until "the full number of the Gentiles" has come in (v. 25b).[228]
c. The Deliverer, the Messiah himself, will turn all ungodliness away from his people when he returns (26b–27).[229]

So the time will come, though it seems that Israel's fate will change not simply through "regular" mission work but by means of God's own mighty intervention.[230] For sure, it is not revealed how he will fulfill his plans in the end.[231]

Though already treated in passing, vv. 26b–27 depict the turning point for the history of salvation with a scriptural argument:

Ἥξει ἐκ Σιὼν ὁ ῥυόμενος, ἀποστρέψει ἀσεβείας ἀπὸ Ἰακώβ. Καὶ αὕτη αὐτοῖς ἡ παρ᾽ ἐμοῦ διαθήκη, ὅταν ἀφέλωμαι τὰς ἁμαρτίας αὐτῶν.

"The Deliverer will come from Zion, he will banish ungodliness from Jacob"; "and this will be my covenant with them when I take away their sins."

Once again, two Old Testament passages are combined. In this case, they are both from Isaiah: 59:20–21a in vv. 26b–27a and 27:9 in v. 27b. The text follows LXX. Hence it says that the Deliverer will come and ἀποστρέψει ἀσεβείας ἀπὸ Ἰακώβ ("turn ungodliness away from Jacob") instead of "to those in Jacob who turn from transgression" (but still due to God's goodness as in Isa. 59:21b). The last clause in the quotation is then adapted to suit the previous. Accordingly, it is plural (*"their* sins" [τὰς ἁμαρτίας αὐτῶν, in keeping with "my covenant with *them*"]), not singular ("his [= Jacob's] sins").[232] Further, Paul himself changes the phrase "to Zion" (BH), or "for Zion's sake" (ἕνεκεν Σιων; LXX), to "from Zion" (ἐκ Σιών). Presumably, he does this in order to communicate the Old Testament understanding of salvation, which stems from Zion. Especially Ps. 50:2 is relevant because it describes how God shines forth out of Zion. The context speaks of his coming (v. 3) in consort with the rising and setting of the sun (v. 1), just as Isa. 59:19–20 (LXX) does.[233] In addition, the phrase "from Zion" is also found, for example, in Ps. 14:7 and 53:6 with the hope of "salvation for Israel," a desire that relates them to Isa. 27:9 and 59:20–21 (then coalesces in Rom. 11:26b–27). What is more, both the psalmist and the prophet direct their words to "Jacob," another common feature between them.[234] All things considered, it seems as if Paul finds his Scripture quotations from different sources. He intentionally compiles associated traditions into a multifaceted totality. In his exposition, Isaiah's prophecies are explained by the prayers of the Psalms.[235]

The one who, according to Isa. 59:20, will come is the Lord (Jahve). In Rom. 11:26, the text is applied to Christ himself (see above; 9:5).[236] The word ὁ ῥυόμενος ("Deliverer") has a strong eschatological content and refers to his return (1 Thess. 1:10; cf. Rom. 7:24).[237] The future tense of the verb ἥξει ("shall come") includes the same nuance.[238] On doomsday, Christ will come from Zion, which refers to either the "earthly" Jerusalem (Matt. 23:39; Acts 1:11) or the "heavenly" Jerusalem (Gal. 4:26; Heb. 12:22; Rev. 3:12).[239] At that moment, he will cleanse his people by turning ungodliness away from them and forgiving their sins. Simply put, he still keeps to his Messianic program and does not act as a political Messiah. He introduces a *spiritual* renewal (which for certain has practical and concrete consequences). The language here by its very nature reminds of the presentation of Abraham's (and David's) justification in chapter 4. The adjective ἀσεβής ("ungodly") and the term αἱ ἁμαρτίαι ("sins") in plural (commonly in singular in the Pauline Epistles) are found there (vv. 5, 7).[240] At Christ's Parousia, all Israel will be saved in the same way as everybody else—namely, through faith in the gospel (see above). Their transgressions will be forgiven and righteousness counted as theirs in agreement with the theme of Romans (1:16–17).[241] The promise of a new covenant in Jer. 31:31–34, which the Scripture quotation "my covenant with them" in v. 27 clearly alludes to, will be realized in Israel. The hardening of the people only has a temporary character (cf. the context for Isa. 27:9 and 59:20, which both speak about the end of God's punishment sometime in the future).[242]

On occasion, the question arises of whether there is a contradiction between the two statements "*all* Israel will be saved" (chapter 11) and "only a *remnant* of [Israel] will be saved" (chapter 9). Yet it has already been shown above that the phrase "all Israel" should not be understood in a *diachronic* but in a *synchronic* way; in other words, it does not embrace all Israelites at all times but those Israelites living at the end of world history. Therefore, all Israel in fact represents a remnant of Israel. Further, chapter 9 strictly refers to the *spiritual* Israel, while chapter 11 relates to the *ethnic* Israel, which later on, after an intervention by the Messiah himself, becomes spiritual. Consequently, there is no foundation for a contradiction between the two perspectives. The argumentation is stringent and consistent throughout.[243]

In short, finally the anguished question becomes silent: "Who has believed what he has heard from us?" (10:16). Astonishingly, all Israel believes and is saved (11:26)! At their salvation, only thanksgiving and praise remain. The next passage shows one good example.

(7) 11:33–36

The verses conclude the entire argumentation in chapters 9–11 and even chapters 1–11.[244] The doxology in v. 36b corresponds to the eulogy in 9:5. Considering that fact, praise of God takes a dominant place in the presentation. He is praised already in the beginning of chapter 9 and over again in the end of chapter 11. The structural arrangement works well with the general theme, which focuses on the question of the Jewish people, as the term *Jew* denotes "the one who praises the Lord" (Gen. 29:35).[245]

Verses 33–36 are made up of three stanzas, each of which have three units:

> a. v. 33 (three exclamations relating to God's wise salvation historical plan),
> b. vv. 34–35 (three rhetorical questions pertaining to man's inability to understand God's wise salvation historical plan), and
> c. v. 36 (three short expressions with different prepositions that all emphasize that God is absolutely sovereign in his wise salvation historical plan).[246]

The doxology as a whole circles around the unfathomable in the Lord's good counsel, as it is proclaimed in the Old Testament and treated in chapters 9–11.

Exclamations like "oh" (ὦ) and "how" (ὡς) in v. 33 are characteristic facets for hymnal and liturgical texts. The condensed phrases praise God's "riches and wisdom and knowledge," "unsearchable [. . .] judgments," and "inscrutable [. . .] ways." Each of them briefly summarizes some significant aspect of the previous argumentation in regard to Holy Scripture:

> • πλούτου ("riches"), God's grace toward all sinners (cf. v. 12)
> • σοφίας ("wisdom"), God's salvation plan pertaining to Jews and Gentiles (cf. especially vv. 30–32)
> • γνώσεως ("knowledge"), mainly God's election (cf. especially v. 2; see also 8:29)

- τὰ κρίματα—αἱ ὁδοί ("judgments" and "ways"), God's sovereign guidance of history (cf. vv. 11–12, 30–32). Both "how" phrases are parallel in their structure: predicative adjective—definitive article—subject—possessive pronoun (furthermore, both predicative adjectives begin with the same root: *anex*-).[247]

No one can understand the depth that characterizes God's sovereign actions in agreement with v. 33. He rises above all human comprehension. Not even the Old Testament as such discloses the hidden mysteries written there. It will be "unveiled" only due to the gospel (see 1:2–4, 16:25–26).[248] Yet every now and then, a special revelation is necessary to shed more light on certain obscure marks of salvation history. Patently, as an apostle, Paul himself has received an insight beyond measure into God's mystery (11:25–27). His exceptional knowledge, as expected, exceeds general knowledge of Holy Scripture—but he does not in the least empty the well of truth (cf. 1 Cor. 2:6–16).[249]

The questions in vv. 34–35 are found in Isa. 40:13–14 and Job 41:2. They seem to refer back to the three previous genitive nouns (v. 33) in chiastic order:[250]

Τίς γὰρ ἔγνω νοῦν Κυρίου;

"Who has known the mind of the Lord?" (v. 34a) corresponds to the exclamation regarding God's knowledge (γνῶσις).

ἢ τίς σύμβουλος αὐτοῦ ἐγένετο;

"Who has been his counselor?" (v. 34b) coincides with the proclamation concerning God's wisdom.

ἢ τίς προέδωκεν αὐτῷ, καὶ ἀνταποδοθήσεται αὐτῷ;

"Who has given a gift to him that he might be repaid?" (v. 35) finally retells the declaration in respect of God's riches.[251]

Apparently, the last question deals with the theme of Romans: justification by faith, which is based not on any human merits but only on God's grace. The final doxology in v. 36 no doubt revolves around the same theme and exalts him alone—from which, through which, and to which all things are[252]—not the least pertaining to the doctrine of justification.[253] If it is so, the apostolic argumentation is not finished until the Creator, instead of humanity created by him, has been highly praised.[254]

Ergo, a thorough reading of chapters 9–11 is over. Next, chapters 12–15, the paraenetic part of Romans, are treated in short according to the definition of the task at the outset.

Application for Practical Life

To further solidify Paul's way of exposing Scripture, it is worth taking another look at his conclusions for practical life in the church. A few examples are enough.

(1) Love as the Fulfillment of the Law

Concerning the Pauline interpretation of the law, the focal question is this: Is the law still valid? And if it is, is then the entire law or only a certain part of the law valid? The starting point for our study is Rom. 13:9–10:

> For the commandments, "You shall not commit adultery, You shall not murder, You shall not steal, You shall not covet," and any other commandment, are summed up in this word: "You shall love your neighbor as yourself." Love does no wrong to a neighbor; therefore love is the fulfilling of the law.

As a comparison, Gal. 5:14 is also quoted:

> For the whole law is fulfilled in one word: "You shall love your neighbor as yourself."

In the paraenetic parts of his letters, Paul thus concentrates on love of one's neighbor. He obviously presumes that the first commandment (love toward God) has already been fulfilled in and through faith (cf. Rom. 8:28). What does it mean in this context that love is the fulfillment of the law (or "the second tablet")?

Paul does not expect that Gentile Christians be circumcised and live according to the Jewish festival calendar or pay for temple sacrifices. On the other hand, he does not anywhere make a distinction between the current moral law and the extinct cult law even though such a distinction is actually valid.[255] In fact, Paul argues that all the rules in the entire law are included in the commandment to love. His thought pattern is reflected as follows.

Christians fulfill the cult law by offering their bodies (in love) "as [. . .] living sacrifice[s], holy and acceptable to God." It is their "spiritual worship" (Rom. 12:1; λογικὴ λατρεία). Since their entire lives will be consecrated to God, they do not even need any dietary rules or regulations about special festivals with ritual washing because love covers them all.

In the Epistle to the Philippians, Paul goes on to use similar language in dealing with his apostolic office. There he speaks about his own blood as a drink offering that will finally be poured "over the sacrifice" (ἐπὶ τῇ θυσίᾳ) when he does his "temple service" (λειτουργία) for the Philippians, or in their place—a clear reference to their economic support (cf. 4:10ff.), which in practice enabled his mission, "a sacrificial liturgy" (2:17).

Likewise, Christians fulfill the law of circumcision by letting their *hearts* be circumcised "by the Spirit," not "by the letter" (Rom. 2:28–29). It is explicitly through the Holy Spirit that "God's love" (subjective genitive) is poured into the *hearts* of the Christians (5:5). The Spirit wakens in them a love directed back at God and neighbor (15:30). Christians, who serve through the Spirit of God, are counted as the circumcised (Phil. 3:3). The expression of "serving through the Spirit of God" (οἱ πνεύματι θεοῦ λατρεύοντες) refers back to "spiritual service" (λογικὴ λατρεία) in Rom. 12:1 (see above).[256]

Hence Christians need not keep all the Old Testament rules literally "in the flesh" but "in the Spirit." By sacrificing themselves and by circumcising their hearts, it is with more than enough that they fulfill those regulations, which they no longer practice anymore according to the "normal" Jewish convention. Yet it is not a question of an idealistic Christendom, since Paul urges his readers to place their *bodies* in the service of righteousness. Probably he as a former Pharisee has "Christianized" his former ideal to extend the purity rules of the clergy to take place even in an ordinary person's daily life.

Furthermore, love should not be classified as just one special virtue among others. Rather, it indicates that Christ works in the Christians. He lives in and through them. In Rom. 13, love means "put[ting] on the armor of light" (v. 12), which is identical to "put[ting] on the Lord Jesus Christ" (v. 14). He (or his Spirit) dwells in Christians and fights against the flesh (8:9–11). They are crucified with him in order to walk with him "in newness of life" (6:4, 6:8, 6:10–11). In Gal. 5, a similar thought is found (vv. 16–25). The Christians live no longer, but Christ lives in them (2:20). A personal relationship to him defines their acting in love.[257]

(2) The Apostle as a Representative of Jesus Christ

In addition, through his apostolic office, Paul sees himself fulfilling Old Testament prophecies. For example, in Rom. 15:9b–11, he quotes certain selected texts with a Christological application from the Book of Psalms and Deuteronomy:

> As it is written, "Therefore I will praise you among the Gentiles, and sing to your name" [Ps. 18:49]. And again it is said, "Rejoice, O Gentiles, with his people" [Deut. 32:43]. And again, "Praise the Lord, all you Gentiles, and let all the peoples extol him" [Ps. 117:1].

All the quoted Old Testament texts deal with *Christ's* song of praise among the Gentiles and with his exhortation to them to join in his song. Actually, he sang Ps. 117:1 together with his disciples after the Passover meal, in connection with the institution of Lord's Supper on Maundy Thursday (Matt. 26:30; Mark 14:26). But how exactly have the Old Testament prophecies now been fulfilled? The Gentiles have not heard Christ's song of praise! And yet they have. For Paul says in v. 16 about himself that he is Jesus Christ's "liturgist" (λειτουργός; a "priestly steward," a "temple priest," or a "servant") among the Gentiles. Thus Christ sings with his mouth![258] The apostolic office is that highly esteemed. As a messenger, the apostle represents his Sender (see also 10:14),[259] an understanding that goes back to the teachings of the Evangelists (Matt. 10:40; Luke 10:16; John 13:20). Once again, the importance and significance of a personal relationship to Christ appears in the whole letter.

Evaluation of the Results

On the whole, not every Old Testament allusion or quotation in Romans has been considered above (which would completely break the limits of the analysis). Yet the outlines for the scriptural argumentation are delineated to a great extent. The main thesis in 1:16–17, the general rules for interpretation especially seen from the perspective of chapters 1–8, the focus on chapters 9–11, and the application to practical life in chapters 12–15 show the directions for Paul's hermeneutics. His reading of the Old Testament greatly differs from the philological and exegetical research common today. He does not limit himself to analyzing the historical meaning of the biblical texts but sees their actual fulfillment in Christ according to his gospel. Simply put, both philology and exegetics are subordinated to theology.

As a summary, M. Silva maintains as follows:

> There is no evidence that Paul or his contemporaries ever sat down to "exegete" OT texts in a way comparable to what today's seminary students are expected to do—that is, to produce an exposition that focuses on the historical meaning. Nevertheless, many of Paul's actual uses of Scripture are acknowledged by all concerned to be consistent with such a historical meaning.[260]

In other words, the Pauline exegesis is a Christological exposition of the Bible where the original historical setting of the Old Testament is not ignored but serves as an absolutely necessary condition for the interpretation. Similarly, J. R. Wagner concludes,

> The story of God, Israel, and the Gentiles that Paul tells in Romans reflects the dynamic interplay of his foundational convictions, his reading of Israel's scriptures, his labors in mission, and his cultural and

historical contexts. By no stretch of the imagination can Paul said to interpret Isaiah and other scriptural texts in Romans in a detached and disinterested manner. [. . .] And yet, at the same time, the letter to the Romans reveals, perhaps more clearly than any other of Paul's letters, the deep and pervasive influence that Israel's scriptures exert on the shape of his thought and on the contours of his apostolic ministry.[261]

Given that Paul does not stop at a reading that focuses on the historical sense of the texts, he continually looks for a "deeper meaning" (*sensus plenior*) that takes the wider messianic context into account. Here, it is absolutely critical to understand that even the Christological Bible exposition claims to be literal—only seen from the perspective of faith.[262] Christ is really found in the Old Testament. He is, so to speak, interwoven in those texts. The prophecies are fulfilled through him, and in him their message reaches its climax. A purely historical explanation without a close connection to the gospel does not express the whole truth or the core of the truth. Quite the opposite, the hermeneutics of Romans is based on Old Testament exegetics, which affirm faith in Christ and assume his life work, especially his death on the cross on Good Friday and his resurrection on the third day. Where all that is missing, theological research fails, substituting the living kerygma of the Early Church with a philosophical system that can never do justice to the divine revelation.[263]

In Romans, the application of the Christian understanding of Scripture in practice suggests that it is not intended for a theoretical approach that cannot be used in the Church's work and everyday life. On the contrary, the idea of love as the fulfillment of the law and the emphasis on Christ who works through the apostolic office cover all kinds of commonplace conditions. Thus such a theological persuasion will always maintain its relevance.[264]

Further reflections on the importance of the hermeneutics, as depicted in Romans, follow in the next chapter. Accordingly, a short summary of the main results is provided, and some fresh conclusions are drawn.

V
Summary and Conclusions

Summary

The undertaking of this work was to investigate the hermeneutics of Romans, especially the guidelines that affect Pauline interpretation of the Old Testament. To truly come to terms with the issue, a short overview of research history regarding the ideological and philosophical presuppositions of the theological discipline was outlined. Somewhat surprisingly, it revealed that an atheistic undertone characterizes the historical-critical method in general as well as various alternative or additional models. In its deepest sense, the common tendency they share reaches back to the thinking of Immanuel Kant. This has caused a deep crisis in *theology* (in the real meaning of the word) and *theological* research.

Already in his day, Dietrich Bonhoeffer made a new and serious attempt to do justice to the uniqueness of the theological discipline. His main interest concerns the relationship between *Akt* and *Sein* ("faith" and "revelation") from the church's "personal relationship" with Christ. His paradigm at last avoids the atheistic presupposition and reaches a hermeneutic breakthrough, which, however, has been forgotten ever since. The time has come to bring up his thoughts in an academic context.

Even if Bonhoeffer had a correct starting point, it seemed necessary to develop his theses by more closely determining the issue of revelation and its central message. The investigation was then developed in a similar way from the "personal relationship" with Christ.

Here we studied the theme and disposition of Romans, which show the following characteristics:

1. the revelation (Old Testament)
2. the central message of the revelation (justification by faith)
3. the general validity of the revelation for both Jews and Gentiles (the unity of the Church)

All the characteristics here are closely related to the person of Christ. In the deepest sense, he is their content.

The Christological understanding of Scripture in Romans was then presented and expounded with the help of a few relevant guidelines for interpretation: First, the scriptural aspect "promise-fulfillment" was used. Second, typological Bible exposition was utilized. Finally, the Old Testament as a whole was considered as anticipating the New Testament era. The apostolic argumentation is virtually built on those premises.

The importance of the Christological perspective was even more apparent in an in-depth exegesis of chapters 9–11. There, a large number of Old Testament quotations are given exposition. They are related to the person and salvific work of Christ without ignoring or trivializing the original context. Paul's way of doing Old Testament exegesis under such circumstances greatly differs from today's so-called historical-critical Bible research (whether it is liberal or conservative). He does not limit himself to the immanent interpretation of Scripture but sees their actual fulfillment in the gospel "according to the revelation of the mystery that was kept secret for long ages but has now been disclosed" (Rom. 16:25–26).

Lastly, by examples from chapters 12–15, the convincing force of the Christological approach was emphasized in everyday life. Love as the fulfillment of the law means that Christ acts in Christians, and the apostle in his ministry represents Christ. Both notions show how very concretely Paul applies his thoughts on reality. He avoids mutilating theological truths by theorizing them.

The Result in Form of Image

A short overview of the hermeneutics of Romans, especially the determining factors of the apostle's exposition of Scripture, and their application in everyday life has both concretized and completed Bonhoeffer's position. Thus there are three relevant perspectives of revelation, and they firmly point to Christ. The result is graphically shown with an equilateral triangle as follows:

Rom. 9–11: Bible (the Old Testament)

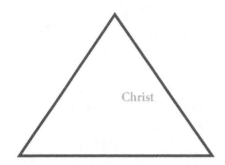

Rom. 1–8: Justification (faith)   Rom. 12–15: Congregation (love)

The figure shows that Christ should be all in all. With his presence, he fills the different aspects of revelation and unites them into one coherent entity. Accordingly, the main units of Romans, chapters 1–8, 9–11, and 12–15, demonstrably appear to full advantage. They are in concert with each other.

In addition, the distinctive "embodiments" of Christ shows the dynamic character of the revelation. There are not merely (necessary) doctrinal statements concerning him and his solidarity with humankind. More precisely, he in his own person represents salvation "to everyone who believes." Further, he rises from the pages of the Old Testament as Mediator between God and the fallen world. Last but not least, he even identifies himself with his congregation, showing his love and compassion through human relationships. In that sense, the church is included in the "happening" of the revelation but not as an autonomous institution. As a whole, the hermeneutics in Romans really opens up new paths forward.

The Hermeneutics of Romans and Academic Research

It would be incorrect to accuse Paul of reading his Bible arbitrarily. There *are* crystal-clear criteria for assessing his exposition of Holy Scripture (see above). He uses his methods—to put it anachronistically for the sake of clarity—"strictly scientifically." But the apostolic exposition is built not on an atheistic (or agnostic) foundation but on the cornerstone, Jesus Christ (cf. Eph. 2:20). In him, the Bible with its diverse content is formed into a towering and richly decorated cathedral, where thanks and praise are continually sung to the glory of God, rather than a church slowly falling into decay and becoming the abandoned ruins from different eras of religious history.

Consequently, the very contentious issue in biblical scholarship does not exclusively concern the question of the historical trustworthiness of the Old Testament accounts. Defending the accuracy of miscellaneous data and facts in the Scripture does not yet entrust the church with an understanding that bears any weighty resemblance to the hermeneutics in Romans. Much more is needed. In the end, the crucial question revolves around whether Christ is to be found in the Old Testament texts. The New Testament kerygma affirms his presence there.

Apparently, herein lies the stumbling stone. Apostolic reading presupposes Christian faith. To truly understand the Old Testament and therefore also the New Testament, or the other way around, the reader already has to believe in Christ as the true fulfillment of Scripture.[1] He is not able to master the revelation with his reason and reasoning, even if it is entirely bound to "an objective world"— more specifically, the biblical texts. Thus the relationship between *Akt* and *Sein* (*Act* and *Being*) maintains the balance in accord with Bonhoeffer's extensive argumentation: in order to know the truth in and through the word, we always already have to be known by the Truth in and through the Word—namely, Christ.[2]

The same discernment also applies to the notion that Christ acts in Christians through love and with Paul in his apostolic office. Therein, we are drawn into the "action" of revelation without having any power over it. God maintains his sovereignty. He continually remains beyond the reach of reason but in contact with the humanity that he has created. Hence biblical research presupposes, even given the practical consequences, close communion with Christ and living faith in him.[3] Yet academic theology in general lacks an understanding for this fact. Accordingly, we have to ask ourselves if the exegetical results are to be told from the lectern in a scholastic context or rather from the pulpit within the sphere of the church. Surely, it would not be recommended to separate the lectern and the pulpit but dedicate them both to the gospel, which God "promised beforehand through his prophets in the holy Scriptures" (Rom. 1:2).[4]

The Hermeneutic Circle

Understanding presumes contact between the author (speaker) and the reader (hearer) in the form of a text (a speech) that has a certain message.[5] If any of these aspects are missing, communication will fail. Effective information goes from the sender to the receiver and gives new or deepened insight.

The letter to the Romans works excellently in such a process of understanding. It includes all the abovementioned aspects in a communication. The apostle of the Lord writes a letter—which is based on the word that the Lord has spoken—to the congregation in the Lord in order to present the Lord "for righteousness to everyone who believes" (10:4). Apparently, Christ is at the center. He is not only the content of the message, but the Old Testament as Holy Scripture in its entirety and read in agreement with the gospel has his authority. In addition, he is hidden behind both the sender and the receiver. Actually, no part of the communication process works without him! So the hermeneutics of Romans inevitably presupposes that Christ lives and acts in the church. Faith in him and in his resurrection is necessary. Here we see an absolute paradox: in order to understand, one has to understand what one cannot understand. In the end, the hermeneutic circle leads to—nowhere![6] Is there, then, no way out of this? Yes, there truly is one: he who once said, "I am the way."[7]

Criteria for the Later Canon Process

Furthermore, it is of utmost interest that the later canon process actually follows a similar criteria to that which the hermeneutics of

Romans indicate. In order for an ancient writing to be accepted as having eternal divine authority, it had to fulfill the following—not in any way easy—demands:

1. apostolic origin
2. conformity with the Old Testament
3. conformity with the "rule of faith" (*regula fidei*)
4. general usage in the congregations[8]

To be sure, Romans has, even according to the most radical biblical criticism, apostolic origin (1). It represents argumentation in accordance with the Old Testament (2), its central message of justification is included in the rule of faith (3), and the spiritual guidance as a whole manifests itself in the sphere of the congregations (4). Here it is worth paying attention to the last point. The involvement of the church in the forming of canon is often seen as proof that she ultimately defined the limits of canon or that because of her significant contribution, a normative collection of writings was ever brought about. Hence canon and its authority are relativized. But judging from the hermeneutics of Romans, this is not the case. The involvement of the church in the forming of canon was *theologically* necessary. The church as the body of Christ, not as a human institution, represents Christ and has as his voice in the world made her contribution to the gathering and putting together of canon. It would be strange if she did *not!* Then she would have failed. In the deepest sense, the church has established the width and limits of canon explicitly given that the body and word of Christ always belong together. If she no longer knows his voice, she is surely no longer alive. Put simply, in the process of forming canon, it is not about the church as an independent actor but about the church that has been created by the same word, which has been entrusted to her. This is the only way to guarantee the right relationship between *Act* and *Being*, or to obstruct every attempt to rule over revelation in one way or another.[9]

An Ecumenical Perspective

The hermeneutics of Romans is depicted as a single unity, where the different parts and features are not to be overemphasized or set against each other. Admittedly, throughout the lengthy history of the church, some forms of one-sidedness have emerged. Without generalization, one may suggest that the church's status or hegemony is easily stressed too much within Roman Catholicism, either through the hierarchy of the office structure or due to the merits of those involved. Instead, within the Reformed spirituality, a quite narrow-minded perspective on the Bible as merely a law book prevails. Alternatively, in the Lutheran theology, the doctrine of justification is often streamlined to an almost mathematical proposition, which concerns sinners provided that they only in their mind take it most seriously. Such simplifications or those that are similar do not do justice to the well-balanced hermeneutics of Romans. Its different aspects are not to be allowed to compete with each other but should complete each other in harmony. Else we lose sight of the entirety.

In addition, the so-called evangelical circles exert remarkable influence today, especially in Anglo-Saxon countries. They defend the authority of the Bible and often have an interconfessional profile. Slowly but surely, their number has increased, which is positive in itself. Yet at the same time, their inner identity and harmony have more and more fallen apart. Currently, it is hard to identify exactly what "evangelical" really stands for. For that reason, some relevant guidelines should be determined and expanded with the intention to establish common doctrinal basis. In the quest for consensus, the hermeneutics of Romans has much to offer. All who have ears to hear and submit in humility to the biblical message are on the right path even if complete unity cannot be immediately achieved.[10]

Very last, in theological research, the theological dimension must always prevail. For this reason, atheistic or agnostic methods do not have any place in theology: the doctrine of God cannot be treated as if God does not exist. Theology has to remain theological! Because the texts that biblical research mainly deals with explicitly originate from the *Church's* Bible, it is completely untenable if the Church's faith is ignored. Indeed, the apostolic kerygma asserts that "everything written about me [Christ] in the Law of Moses and the

Prophets and the Psalms must be fulfilled" (Luke 24:44). One who settles on another starting point in the name of academic procedure does not engage in theological studies in the deepest sense of the term but has Marcion as his Master—instead of Jesus of Nazareth.

Glory be
to the Father and the Son and the Holy Spirit,
as it was in the beginning, is now, and will be forever.

List of Literature

The abbreviations used in the list of literature refer as a rule to the list of abbreviations of S. Schwertner (TRE). Berlin 1993.

Primary Literature

The Apocrypha and Pseudepigrapha of the Old Testament in English
With introductions and critical and explanatory notes to the several books, I–II. Edited in conjunction with many scholars by R. H. Charles. Oxford 1963–64 (= 1913).

The Aramaic Bible
Targum Neofiti 1: Exodus. Trans., with introduction and apparatus, by M. McNamara; notes by R. Hayward. Collegeville 1994.

Bauer, W.
A Greek-English Lexicon of the New Testament and Other Early Christian Literature. Based on Walter Bauer's *Griechisch-Deutsches Wörterbuch zu den Schriften des Neues Testament und der übrigen urchristlichen Literatur*. Revised and edited by F. W. Danker. Chicago ³2011.

Bauer, W.
Griechisch-Deutsches Wörterbuch zu den Schriften des Neuen Testaments und der frühchristlichen Literatur. Ed. by K. and B. Aland. Berlin ⁶1988.

Bible
The Holy Bible. New International Version. 1984.

Biblia Hebraica Stuttgartensia
Editio funditus renovata. Ed. by K. Elliger, W. Rudolph et H. P. Rüger. Ed. quarta emend. Stuttgart 1990.

Blass, F.—Debrunner, A.
  Grammatik des neutestamentlichen Griechisch. Bearbeitet von
  F. Rehkopf. Göttingen [18]2001.
Bornemann, E.—Risch, E.
  Griechische Grammatik. Frankfurt am Main [2]2012 (= 1978).
Conybeare, F. C.—Stock, S. G.
  Grammar of Septuagint Greek. With Selected Readings,
  Vocabularies, and Updated Indexes.
Jastrow, M.
  A Dictionary of the Targumim, the Talmud Babli, Talud
  Yerushalmi and the Midrashic Literature. New York 2004.
Josephus
  Josephus with an English Translation. Ed. and trans. by H. S. J.
  Thackeray, R. Marcus, A. Wikgren, and L. H. Feldman. 9 vol-
  umes. LCL. London 1956–69.
Konkordanz zum Novum Testamentum Graece
  von Nestle-Aland, 26. Auflage und zum Greek New Testament,
  3rd edition. Ed. by Institut für neutestamentliche Textforschung
  und vom Rechenzentrum der Universität Münster unter
  besonderer Mitwirkung von H. Bachmann and W. A. Slaby.
  Berlin [3]1987.
Mishna
  S. Talmud.
Muraoka, T.
  A Greek-English Lexicon of the Septuagint.
  Louvain—Paris—Walpole 2009.
Muraoka, T.
  A Syntax of Septuagint Greek. Louvain—Paris—Bristol 2016.
A New English Translation of the Septuagint
  Oxford 2007.
Novum Testamentum Graece
  Based on the work of Eberhard and Erwin Nestle. Ed. by B. and
  K. Aland, J. Karavidopoulos, C. M. Martini, and B. M. Metzger.
  Stuttgart [28]2012.
Nyberg, H. S.
  Hebreisk grammatik. Stockholm [2]1972 (= 1952).
Philo

Philo with an English Translation. Ed. and trans. by F. H. Colson
and G. H. Whitaker. 10 volumes (and 2 supplementary volumes). LCL. London 1929–63.

Septuaginta
Id est Vetus Testamentum Graece iuxta LXX interpretes I–II.
Ed. A. Rahlfs. Stuttgart 1979.
Vetus Testamentum Graecum. Auctoritate Academiae
Scientiarum Gottingensis Editum. Göttingen 1931.

Talmud
Der babylonische Talmud I–IX. Mit Einschluss der vollstaendi-
gen Mišnah. Ed. by nach der ersten, zensurfreien bomb-
ergschen Ausgabe (Venedig 1520–23), nebst Varianten der
spaeteren, von S. Lorja, J. Berlin, J. Sirhes u.aa. rev. Ausgaben
und der muenchener Talmudhandschrift, moeglichst sinn- und
wortgetreu uebersetzt und mit kurzen Erklaerungen versehen
von L. Goldschmidt. Haag 1933–35.
*Der Jerusalemische Talmud in seinen haggadischen
Bestandtheilen: Zum ersten Male in's Deutsche übertragen von A.*
Wünsche. Hildesheim 1967 (= Zürich 1880).
The Talmud of Babylonia: An American Translation
Volume 1, *Tractate Berakhot.* Trans. by J. Neusner. Chico 1984.
Volume 29, *Tractate Menahot I–III.* Trans. by J. Neusner.
Atlanta 1991.
Volume 36, *Tractate Niddah I–II.* Trans. by J. Neusner. Atlanta
1990.

The Tosefta
Trans. by J. Neusner. New Jersey—New York 1977–86.

Secondary Literature

Aageson, J. W. 1986	Scripture and Structure in the Development of the Argument in Romans 9–11. *CBQ* 48, 265–89.
Aageson, J. W. 1987	Typology, Correspondence, and the Application of Scripture in Romans 9–11. *JSNT* 31, 51–72.

Althaus, P. 1958   *Das sogenannte Kerygma und der his-*
                                 torische Jesus. Gütersloh.

Att tolka bibeln i dag.   *Att tolka bibeln i dag: Påvliga bibelkom-*
1995   *missionens dokument om bibeltolkningen*
                                 i kyrkan (1993). Katolsk dokumenta-
                                 tion 22. Uppsala.

Badenas, R. 1985   *Christ the End of the Law: Romans 10,4*
                                 in Pauline Perspective. JSNT suppl.
                                 Series 10. Sheffield.

Barrett, C. K. 1977   Romans 9.30—10.21: Fall and
                                 Responsibility of Israel. *Die Israelfrage*
                                 nach Röm 9–11. Ed. by L. de
                                 Lorenzi. Monographische Reihe von
                                 "Benedictina." Biblisch-ökumenische
                                 Abteilung. Rom, 99–130.

Barth, K. ³1945   *Die kirchliche Dogmatik.* Volume 2,
                                 Die Lehre vom Wort Gottes.
                                 Prolegomena zur kirchlichen Dogmatik.
                                 Zollikon-Zürich.

Bayer, O. 2002   *Vernunft ist Sprache. Hamanns*
                                 Metakritik Kants. With Unter Mitarbeit
                                 von B. Gleede and U. Moustakas.
                                 Stuttgart.

Beker, J. 1984   *Paul the Apostle: The Triumph of God in*
                                 Life and Thought. Philadelphia (= 1980).

Berger, K. 1990   *Gottes einziger Ölbaum.* Betrachtungen
                                 zum Römerbrief. Stuttgart.

Bokedal, T. 2005   *The Scriptures and the Lord: Formation*
                                 and Significance of the Christian Biblical
                                 Canon. A Study in Text, Ritual and
                                 Interpretation. Lund.

Bonhoeffer, D. 1988   *Akt und Sein: Transzendentalphilosophie*
                                 und Ontologie in der systematischen
                                 Theologie. Ed. by H-R. Reuter.
                                 München.

Bonhoeffer, D. 1996   *Act and Being: Transcendental Philosophy and Ontology in Systematic Theology*. Trans. by H. M. Rumscheidt. Ed. by W. W. Floyd Jr. Dietrich Bonhoeffer Works, volume 2. Minneapolis.

Brandenburger, E. 1985   Paulinische Schriftauslegung in der Kontroverse um das Verheißungswort Gottes (Röm 9). *ZThK* 82, 1–47.

Brown, R. E. 1955   *The* Sensus Plenior *of Sacred Scripture*. Baltimore.

Bultmann, R. 1988   *Neues Testament und Mythologie: Das Problem der Entmythologisierung der neutestamentlichen Verkündigung*. Originally published in 1941. Ed. by E. Jüngel. Beiträge zur evangelischen Theologie 96. München.

Carson, D. A. 1986   Recent Developments in the Doctrine of Scripture. *Hermeneutics, Authority, and Canon*. Ed. by D. A. Carson and J. D. Woodbridge. Grand Rapids, 1–48.

Carson, D. A. 1996   *The Gagging of God: Christianity Confronts Pluralism*. Leicester.

Carson, D. A. 1997   New Testament Theology. *Dictionary of the Later New Testament and Its Developments*. Ed. by R. P. Martin and P. H. Davids. Downers Grove—Leicester.

Carson, D. A. 2004   Mystery and Fulfillment: Toward a More Comprehensive Paradigm of Paul's Understanding of the Old and the New. *Justification and Variegated Nomism*, volume 2, *The Paradoxes of Paul*. Ed. by D. A. Carson, P. T. O'Brien, and M. A. Seifrid. WUNT 2:181. Tübingen, 393–436.

Carson, D. A.—Moo,   *An Introduction to the New Testament.*
D. J.—Morris, L. 1992   Grand Rapids.

Clements, R. E. 1980   "A Remnant Chosen by Grace" (Romans
                             11:5): The Old Testament Background
                             and Origin of the Remnant Concept.
                             *Pauline Studies: Essays Presented to F. F.
                             Bruce on His 70th Birthday.* Ed. by D. A.
                             Hagner and M. J. Harris. Exeter, 106–21.

Cranfield, C. E. B. 1981   *A Critical and Exegetical Commentary
                             on the Epistle to the Romans.* Volume 2,
                             *Commentary on Romans IX–XVI and
                             Essays.* ICC. Edinburgh (= 1979).

Cranfield, C. E. B. 1982   *A Critical and Exegetical Commentary
                             on the Epistle to the Romans.* Volume 1,
                             *Introduction and Commentary on Romans
                             I–VIII.* ICC. Edinburgh (= 1975).

Davies, W. D. 1977–78   Paul and the People of Israel. *NTS* 24,
                             4–39.

Dunn, J. D. G. 1988a   *Romans 1–8.* WBC 38_A. Dallas.

Dunn, J. D. G. 1988b   *Romans 9–16.* WBC 38_B. Dallas.

Dunn, J. D. G. 2000   Scholarly Methods in the Interpretation
                             of the Gospels. *Auslegung der
                             Bibel in orthodoxer und westlicher
                             Perspektive.* Akten des west-östlichen
                             Neutestamentler/innen-Symposiums
                             von Neamt vom 4.-11. September 1998.
                             Ed. by J. D. G. Dunn, H. Klein, U. Luz,
                             and V. Mihoc. WUNT 130. Tübingen,
                             105–21.

Eastman, S. G. 2017   *Paul and the Person. Reframing Paul's
                             Anthropology.* Grand Rapids.

Ellis, E. E. 1978   Exegetical Patterns in 1 Corinthians
                             and Romans. *Prophecy and
                             Hermeneutic in Early Christianity:
                             New Testament Essays.* Grand Rapids,
                             213–20.

Ellis, E. E. 1991   *The Old Testament in Early Christianity.* WUNT 54. Tübingen.

Erlandsson, S. 1971   Bibeln och vetenskapen. *Ditt ord är sanning: En handbok om Bibeln tillägnad David Hedegård. Biblicums skriftserie nr 2.* Uppsala, 132–36.

Evans, C. A. 1984   Paul and the Hermeneutics of "True Prophecy": A Study of Romans 9–11. *Bib* 65, 560–70.

Flückiger, F. 1955   Christus, des Gesetzes τέλος. *TZ* 11, 153–57.

Gabel, J. B.—Wheeler, C. B.—York, A. D. 2000   *The Bible as Literature. An Introduction.* Oxford.

Gardner, J. 1999   *Sofies värld: Översättning av M. Eriksson.* Falun.

Goppelt, L. 1939   *Typos: Die typologische Deutung des Alten Testaments im Neuen.* Gütersloh.

Goppelt, L. 1981a   *Theologie des Neuen Testaments.* Ed. by J. Roloff. Göttingen.

Goppelt, L. 1981b   *Theology of the New Testament.* Volume 1. Trans. by J. E. Alsup. Ed. by J. Roloff. Grand Rapids.

Gräßer, E. 1981   Zwei Heilswege? Zum theologischen Verhältnis von Israel und Kirche. *Kontinuität und Einheit. Für F. Mußner.* Ed. by P-G. Müller and W. Stenger. Freiburg, 411–29.

Grindheim, S. 2005   *The Crux of Election: Paul's Critique of the Jewish Confidence in the Election of Israel.* WUNT 2:202. Tübingen.

Gruenler, R. G. 1991   *Meaning and Understanding: The Philosophical Framework of Biblical Interpretation.* Foundations of Contemporary Interpretation 2. Grand Rapids.

Hägglund, B. ²1963   *Teologins historia: En dogmhistorisk översikt*. Lund.

Hägglund, B. 2011   *Kunskapsteori och metafysik i teologin. En idéhistorisk tillbakablick*. Lund.

Hahn, F. 1982   Zum Verständnis von Römer 11.26a: "... und so wird ganz Israel gerettet werden." *Paul and Paulinism: Essays in Honour of C. K. Barrett*. London, 221–34.

Hahn, F. 2002   *Theologie des Neuen Testaments*. Volume 2, *Die Einheit des Neuen Testaments*. Thematische Darstellung. Tübingen.

Harrington, D. J. 1992   *Paul on the Mystery of Israel*. Zacchaeus Studies: New Testament. Collegeville.

Harris, H. 1990   *The Tübingen School: A Historical and Theological Investigation of the School of F. C. Baur*. With a new preface by the author and a foreword by E. Earle Ellis. Leicester (= 1975).

Hays, R. B. 1989   *Echoes of Scripture in the Letters of Paul*. New Haven—London.

Henttonen, K. 1997   *Voiko sen tehdä toisinkin? Diakoniatieteen lähtökohdat ja valinnat. Lahden ammattikorkeakoulun julkaisu-sarja C*. Lahti.

Hester, J. D. 2004   Review of L. Thurén, *Derhetorizing Paul. JBL* 123, 171–77.

Hirsch, S. R. 1978   *The Psalms*. Jerusalem—New York.

Hofius, O. 1989a   Gesetz und Evangelium nach 2. Korinther 3. *Paulusstudien*. WUNT 51. Tübingen, 75–120.

Hofius, O. 1989b   Das Evangelium und Israel. Erwägungen zu Römer 9–11. *Paulusstudien*. WUNT 51. Tübingen, 175–202.

Hübner, H. 1984   *Gottes Ich und Israel: Zum*
                         Schriftgebrauch des Paulus in Römer
                         9–11. FRLANT 136. Göttingen.

Hübner, H. 1990   *Biblische Theologie des Neuen*
                         Testaments. Volume 1, *Prologomena.*
                         Göttingen.

Hvalvik, R. 1990   A "Sonderweg" for Israel. A
                         Critical Examination of a Current
                         Interpretation of Romans 11.25–27.
                         JSNT 38, 87–107.

Jäger, P. 1905   Das "atheistische Denken" der neueren
                         Theologie. *Christliche Welt* 25,
                         577–82.

Jeanrond, W. G. 1991   Biblical Criticism and Theology: Toward
                         a New Biblical Theology. *Radical*
                         Pluralism and Truth: David Tracy and
                         the Hermeneutics of Religion. Ed. by
                         W. G. Jeanrond and J. L. Rike. New York,
                         38–48.

Jeremias, J. 1977   Einige vorwiegend sprachliche
                         Beobachtungen zu Röm 11, 25–36. *Die*
                         Israelfrage nach Röm 9–11. Ed. by L. de
                         Lorenzi. Monographische Reihe von
                         "Benedictina." Biblisch-ökumenische
                         Abteilung. Rom, 193–205.

Jewett, R. 1985   The Law and the Coexistence of Jews
                         and Gentiles in Romans. *Interpr* 39,
                         341–56.

Johnson, D. G. 1984   The Structure and Meaning of
                         Romans 11. *CBQ* 46, 91–103.

Joyce, P. 1994   First among Equals? The Historical-
                         Critical Approach in the Marketplace
                         of Methods. *Crossing the Boundaries:*
                         Essays in Biblical Interpretation in
                         Honour of M. D. Goulder. Ed. by S. E.
                         Porter, P. Joyce, and D. E. Orton.
                         Leiden, 17–27.

Karavidopoulos, I.
2000

Offenbarung und Inspiration der Schrift—Interpretation des Neuen Testaments in der orthodoxen Kirche. *Auslegung der Bibel in orthodoxer und westlicher Perspektive.* Akten des west-östlichen Neutestamentler/innen-Symposiums von Neamt vom 4.-11. September 1998. Ed. by J. D. G. Dunn, H. Klein, U. Luz, and V. Mihoc. WUNT 130. Tübingen, 157–68.

Käsemann, E. [4]1980

An die Römer. HNT 8a. Tübingen.

Keskitalo, J. 2004

Raamattu kirkon kertomuksena— Raamatun totuusvaatimus valistuksen jälkeisessä postmodernissa maail-massa. *Raamattu ja kirkon usko tänään: Synodaalikirja 2004.* Ed. by M. Hytönen. Kirkon tutkimuskeskuksen julkai-suja 87. Tampere, 72–89.

Kim, S. 2002

Paul and the New Perspective: Second Thoughts on the Origin of Paul's Gospel. Grand Rapids.

Koch, D.-A. 1986

Die Schrift als Zeuge des Evangeliums: Untersuchungen zur Verwendung und zum Verständnis der Schrift bei Paulus. BHTh 69. Tübingen.

Kuss, O. 1978

Der Römerbrief. Dritte Lieferung (Röm 8,19 bis 11,36). Regensburg.

Laato, T. 1991

Paulus und das Judentum. Anthropologische Erwägungen. Åbo.

Laato, T. 1995

Paul and Judaism: An Anthropological Approach. Atlanta.

Laato, T. 1997

Justification According to James: A Comparison with Paul. *TrinJ* 18, 43–84.

Laato, T. 2002

De Ignorantia Christi: Zur Parusieverzögerung in den synoptischen Evangelien. Saarijärvi.

Laato, T. 2003   *Rechtfertigung bei Jakobus: Ein Vergleich mit Paulus.* Saarijärvi 2003.

Laato, T. 2004   Paul's Anthropological Considerations: Two Problems. *Justification and Variegated Nomism,* volume 2, *The Paradoxes of Paul.* Ed. by D. A. Carson, P. T. O'Brien, and M. A. Seifrid. WUNT 2:181. Tübingen, 343–59.

Laato, T. 2006   *Romarbrevets hermeneutik. En lärobok för teologer om vetenskaplig metod.* Församlingsfakultetens skriftserie nr 7. Göteborg.

Laato, T. 2008   "God's Righteousness"—Once Again. *The Nordic Paul: Finnish Approaches to Pauline Theology.* Ed. by L. Aejmelaeus and A. Mustakallio. ESCO 374. London—New York, 40–73.

Laato, T. 2009a   Paulus och lagen. *Troen, teksten og konteksten: Festskrift til Torben Kjær.* Hillerød, 212–21.

Laato, T. 2009b   Review of B. D. Smith, *What Must I Do to Be Saved? Paul Parts Company with His Jewish Heritage. ThLZ* 134, 808–10.

Laato, T. 2013   Vaimon siemen, joka rikkipolkee käärmeen pään. *Kristus Vanhassa testamentissa. Vanhan testamentin kristologia.* Helsinki, 290–307.

Laato, T. 2015   Romans as the Completion of Bonhoeffer's Hermeneutics. *JETS* 58 (2015), 709–29.

Laato, T. 2019   The New Quest for Paul: A Critique of the New Perspective on Paul. *The Doctrine on Which the Church Stands or Falls: Justification in Biblical, Theological, Historical, and Pastoral Perspective.* Ed. by M. Barrett. Wheaton, 291–321.

Lampe, P. ²1989   *Die stadtrömischen Christen in*
                                 den ersten beiden Jahrhunderten.
                                 Untersuchungen zur Socialgeschichte.
                                 WUNT 2:18. Tübingen.

Legarth, P. V. 2004   *Jesus är Herren: Studier i nogle aspek-*
                                 ter av Kyrios-kristologien hos Paulus.
                                 MVS 9. Århus.

Lindemann, A. 1982   Die Gerechtigkeit aus dem Gesetz.
                                 Erwägungen zur Auslegung und zur
                                 Textgeschichte von Römer 10 5. *ZNW*
                                 73, 231–50.

Linnemann, E. 1990   *Historical Criticism of the Bible:*
                                 Methodology or Ideology? Trans. by
                                 R. W. Yarbrough. Grand Rapids.

Linnemann, E. 2001   *Biblical Criticism on Trial: How*
                                 Scientific Is "Scientific Theology"? Trans.
                                 by R. Yarbrough. Grand Rapids.

Lohfink, N. ²1967   Zur historisch-kritischen Methode.
                                 Bibelauslegung im Wandel. Ein Exeget
                                 ortet seine Wissenschaft. Frankfurt, 50–75.

Longenecker, B. W.   Different Answers to Different Issues:
1989   Israel, the Gentiles and Salvation
                                 History in Romans 9–11. *JSNT* 36,
                                 95–123.

Longenecker, R. N. ²   *Biblical Exegesis in the Apostolic Period.*
1999   Vancouver.

Lübking, H.-M. 1986   *Paulus und Israel im Römerbrief: Eine*
                                 Untersuchung zu Römer 9–11. EHST
                                 260. Frankfurt am Main.

Ludlow, M. 2003   "Criteria of Canonicity" and the Early
                                 Church. *The Unity of Scripture and the*
                                 Diversity of the Canon. Ed. by J. Barton
                                 and M. Wolter. Berlin—New York, 69–93.

Luther, M. 1960   *Luther's Works.* Volume 35, *Word and*
                                 Sacrament I. Minneapolis.

Luther, M. 2012	*The Bondage of the Will.* Trans. by J. I. Packer and O. R. Johnston. Grand Rapids.
Maier, G. 1971	*Mensch und freier Wille: Nach den jüdischen Religionsparteien zwischen Ben Sira und Paulus.* WUNT 12. Tübingen.
Maier, G. ²1975	*Das Ende der historisch-kritischen Methode.* ABCTeam: Glauben und Denken. Wuppertal (= 1974).
Marshall, I. H. 1982	*Biblical Inspiration.* London.
McLay, R. T. 2003	*The Use of the Septuagint in New Testament Research.* Grand Rapids—Cambridge.
Michel, O. 1929	*Paulus und seine Bibel.* BFChTh 2:18. Gütersloh. (New edition in Darmstadt 1972.)
Michel, O. ⁵1978	*Der Brief an die Römer.* KEK 4. Göttingen.
Minde, H.-J. van der. 1976	*Schrift und Tradition bei Paulus: Ihre Bedeutung und Funktion im Römerbrief.* Paderborn.
Moo, D. J. 1986	The Problem of Sensus Plenior. *Hermeneutics, Authority, and Canon.* Ed. by D. A. Carson and J. D. Woodbridge. Grand Rapids, 175–212.
Moo, D. J. 1996	*The Epistle to the Romans.* NICNT. Grand Rapids—Cambridge.
Moo, D. J. 2004	Israel and the Law in Romans 5–11: Interaction with the New Perspective. *Justification and Variegated Nomism,* volume 2, *The Paradoxes of Paul.* Ed. by D. A. Carson, P. T. O'Brien, and M. A. Seifrid. WUNT 2:181. Tübingen, 185–216.
Morris, L. 1988	*The Epistle to the Romans.* PNTC. Grand Rapids.

Müller, C. 1964   *Gottes Gerechtigkeit und Gottes Volk:*
                                   Eine Untersuchung zu Römer 9–11.
                                   FRLANT 86. Göttingen.

Müller, M.—   Relativ oder absolut Irrtumslos? Zu
Herrmann, G. 2010   Veränderungen in Hermann Sasses
                                   Schriftlehre. *Theologische Handreichung*
                                   und Informationen für Lehre und Praxis
                                   lutherischer Kirche 28 (Nr 4). Ed. by
                                   Dozentenkollegium des Lutherischen
                                   Theologischen Seminars Leipzig.

Murray, J. 1982   *The Epistle to the Romans.* Volume 1,
                                   chapters 1 to 8. Volume 2, chapters 9 to
                                   16. NIC 5. Michigan (= 1968).

Mußner, F. 1977   Christus (ist) des Gesetzes Ende zur
                                   Gerechtigkeit für jeden, der glaubt
                                   (Röm. 10, 4). *Paulus—Apostat oder*
                                   Apostel? Jüdische und christliche
                                   Antworten. Regensburg, 31–44.

Neuer, W. 2002   Introduction to *Die Bibel verstehen:*
                                   Aufsätze zur biblischen Hermeneutik. By
                                   A. Schlatter. Gießen/Basel 2002.

Nygren, A. 1979   *Pauli brev till romarna.* TNT 6.
                                   Stockholm.

Odland S. 1937   *Kommentar till Matteus' Evangelium:*
                                   Översättning från norskan av M. Berglid
                                   och D. Hedegård. Stockholm.

Piper, J. ²1993   *The Justification of God: An Exegetical*
                                   and Theological Study of Romans 9:1–23.
                                   Grand Rapids.

Plag, C. 1969   *Israels Wege zum Heil: Eine*
                                   Untersuchung zu Römer 9 bis 11. AzTh
                                   1:40. Stuttgart.

Ponsot, H. 1982   Et ainsi tout Israel sera sauvé: Rom., XI,
                                   26a. Salut et conversion. *RB* 89, 406–17.

Räisänen, H. 1987 — Römer 9–11: Analyse eines geistigen Ringens. *ANRW* 2 25, 4, 2891–939.

Rengstorf, K. H. 1978 — Das Ölbaum-Gleichnis in Röm 11,16ff. Versuch einer weiterführenden Deutung. *Donum Gentilicium: New Testament Studies in Honour of D. Daube.* Oxford, 127–64.

Rese, M. 1975 — Die Vorzüge Israels in Röm. 9,4f. und Eph. 2,12. Exegetische Anmerkungen zum Thema Kirche und Israel. *ThZ* 31, 211–22.

Rese, M. 1988 — Israel und Kirche in Römer 9. *NTS* 34, 208–17.

Richardson, A. 1966 — *Raamattu tieteen aikakaudella.* Vaasa. (English original: *The Bible in the Age of Science.* London 1961.)

Richmond, J. 1978 — *Ritschl: A Reappraisal. A Study in Systematic Theology.* London.

Roberts, J. J. M. 1995 — Historical-Critical Method, Theology, and Contemporary Exegesis. *Biblical Theology: Problems and Perspectives. In Honor of J. Christiaan Beker.* Ed. by S. J. Kraftchick, C. D. Myers Jr., and B. C. Ollenburger. Nashville, 131–41.

Ruether, R. 1974 — *Faith and Fratricide. The Theological Roots of Anti-Semitism.* New York.

Sanday, W.— Headlam, A. [5]1920 — *A Critical and Exegetical Commentary on the Epistle to the Romans.* ICC 6. Edinburgh (= 1902).

Sanders, E. P. 1977 — *Paul and Palestinian Judaism: A Comparison of Patterns of Religion.* London.

Sanders, E. P. 1983 — *Paul, the Law and the Jewish People.* Philadelphia.

Sänger, D. 1986	Rettung der Heiden und Erwählung Israels. Einige vorläufige Erwägungen zu Römer 11,25–27. *KuD* 32, 99–119.
Sasse, H. 1981	Studien zur Lehre von der Heiligen Schrift (Aus dem Nachlaß). *Sacra Scriptura: Studien zur Lehre von der Heiligen Schrift von H. Sasse.* Ed. by Fr. W. Hopf. Erlangen, 9–199.
Sasse, H. 1995	*Scripture and the Church: Selected Essays of Hermann Sasse.* Ed. by J. J. Kloha and R. R. Feuerhahn. St. Louis.
Schaller, B. 1984	Ἥξει ἐκ Σιὼν ὁ Ῥυόμενος: Zur Textgestalt von Jes 59:20f. in Röm 11:26f. *De Septuaginta. Studies in Honour of J. W. Wevers.* Ed. by A. Pietersma and C. Cox. Mississauga, 201–6.
Schlatter, A. 1905	Atheistische Methoden in der Theologie. *Beiträge zur Förderung christlicher Theologie* 9, 229–50.
Schlatter, A. 2002	*Die Bibel verstehen: Aufsätze zur biblischen Hermeneutik.* Ed. by W. Neuer. Lahr.
Schlier, H. 1977	*Der Römerbrief.* HThK 6. Freiburg.
Schmidt, M. A. 1982	Die Zeit der Scholastik. *Handbuch der Dogmen- und Theologiegeschichte.* Ed. by C. Andersen. Volume 1, *Die Lehrentwicklung im Rahmen der Katholizität.* Göttingen.
Schreiner, T. R. 1998	*Romans.* BECNT 6. Grand Rapids.
Seeberg, R. 1913	*Lehrbuch der Dogmengeschichte. Dritter Band: Die Dogmengeschichte des Mittelalters.* Leipzig.
Seifrid, M. 1985	Paul's Approach to the Old Testament in Rom 10:6–8. *TrinJ* 6 NS, 3–37.

Seifrid, M. 2000   *Christ, Our Righteousness. Paul's*
                            Theology of Justification. NSBT 9.
                            Leicester.

Shum, S.-L. 2002   *Paul's Use of Isaiah in Romans: A*
                            Comparative Study of Paul's Letter
                            to the Romans and the Sibylline and
                            Qumran Sectarian Texts. WUNT 2:156.
                            Tübingen.

Siegert, F. 1985   *Argumentation bei Paulus gezeigt an*
                            Röm 9–11. WUNT 34. Tübingen.

Silva, M. 1992   The New Testament Use of the Old
                            Testament: Text Form and Authority.
                            Scripture and Truth. Ed. by D. A. Carson
                            and J. D. Woodbridge. Grand Rapids
                            (= 1983), 147–65.

Silva, M. 1993   Old Testament in Paul. *Dictionary*
                            of Paul and His Letters. Ed. by G. F.
                            Hawthorne, R. P. Martin, and D. G.
                            Reid. Downers Grove—Leicester,
                            630–42.

Skarsaune, O. 2002   *In the Shadow of the Temple: Jewish*
                            Influences on Early Christianity.
                            Downers Grove.

Spanje, T. E. van. 1999   *Inconsistency in Paul? A Critique of the*
                            Work of Heikki Räisänen. WUNT 2:110.
                            Tübingen.

Stendahl, K. 1976   *Paul among Jews and Gentiles and Other*
                            Essays. Philadelphia.

Stuhlmacher, P. 1971   Zur Interpretation von Römer 11,25–
                            32. *Probleme biblischer Theologie.* G. von
                            Rad zum 70. Geburtstag. Ed. by H. W.
                            Wolff. München, 555–70.

Theißen, G. 1983   *Psychologische Aspekte paulinischer*
                            Theologie. FRLANT 131. Göttingen.

Theißen, G. 2002 — Röm 9–11—eine Auseinandersetzung des Paulus mit Israel und mit sich selbst: Versuch einer psychologischen Auslegung. *Fair Play: Diversity and Conflicts in Early Christianity: Essays in Honour of H. Räisänen.* Ed. by I. Dunderberg, C. Tuckett, and K. Syreeni. Leiden—Boston—Köln, 311–41.

Thurén, J. 1994 — *Roomalaiskirje.* Hämeenlinna.

Thurén, L. 2000 — *Derhetorizing Paul: A Dynamic Perspective on Pauline Theology and the Law.* WUNT 124. Tübingen.

Vanhoozer, K. J. 1998 — *Is There a Meaning in This Text? The Bible, the Reader and the Morality of Literary Knowledge.* Leicester.

Veijola, T. 2004 — Kaanonin synty ja teologinen merkitys. *Raamattu ja kirkon usko tänään: Synodaalikirja 2004.* Ed. by M. Hytönen. Kirkon tutkimuskeskuksen julkaisuja 87. Tampere, 53–71.

Wachler, G. 1984 — *Die Inspiration und Irrtumslosigkeit der Schrift. Eine dogmengeschichtliche und dogmatische Untersuchung zu H. Sasse, Sacra Scriptura.* Biblicums skriftserie nr 4. Uppsala.

Wagner, J. R. 2003 — *Heralds of the Good News: Isaiah and Paul in Concert in the Letter to the Romans.* Leiden.

Walter, N. 1984 — Zur Interpretation von Römer 9–11. *ZThK* 81, 172–95.

Watson, F. 2004 — *Paul and the Hermeneutics of Faith.* London—New York.

Wenz, A. 1996 — *Das Wort Gottes—Gericht und Rettung. Untersuchungen zur Autorität der Heiligen Schrift in Bekenntnis und Lehre der Kirche.* FSÖTh 75. Göttingen.

Wenz, A. 2003 Review of O. Bayer, *Vernunft ist Sprache*. *Lutherische Beiträge* 8, 194–99.

Westerhom, S. 2004a The "New Perspective" at Twenty-Five. *Justification and Variegated Nomism*, volume 2, *The Paradoxes of Paul*. Ed. by D. A. Carson, P. T. O'Brien, and M. A. Seifrid. WUNT 2:181. Tübingen, 1–38.

Westerhom, S. 2004b *Perspectives Old and New on Paul: The "Lutheran" Paul and His Critics*. Grand Rapids—Cambridge.

Wilckens, U. 1980 *Der Brief an die Römer*. 2. Teilband. Röm. 6–11. EKK 6. Köln.

Wilcock, M. 2002 *The Message of Psalms 1–72: Songs for the People of God*. The Bible Speaks Today: Old Testament series. Leicester (= 2001).

Wilk, F. 1998 *Die Bedeutung des Jesajabuches für Paulus*. FRLANT 179. Göttingen.

Wilson, W. T. 1991 *Love without Pretense: Romans 12.9–21 and Hellenistic-Jewish Wisdom Literature*. WUNT 2:46. Tübingen.

Wright, N. T. 1993 *The Climax of the Covenant: Christ and the Law in Pauline Theology*. Minneapolis (= 1991).

Wright, N. T. 2013 *Paul and the Faithfulness of God*. Parts 1 and 2. London.

Notes

I. Introduction

[1] See Dunn 1988a, xvi–xvii.

[2] See, e.g., *Att tolka bibeln i dag* 1995, 22–53.

[3] See especially Gruenler 1991, 21–109. Cf. below.

[4] See, e.g., the discussion and referenced material in Thurén 2000, 3. Also, cf. J. D. Hester's generally positive review (2004, 171–77). He concludes his broad assessment of the current research as follows: "More work needs to be done to show how *rhetorical* approaches help us get at ideology and theology in ways that other approaches (literary, historical-reconstructive, linguistic, sociological) cannot."

[5] The arcane term *hermeneutics* refers to the presuppositions, often bound to certain philosophical theories that direct the whole process of interpretation and usually seek to apply the ancient text's meaning to today's world (being completely dissimilar). Romans has its own hermeneutical premises as well, which are Christological. They necessitate a Christological interpretation of the Old Testament in order for its message for the church to open up (see below).

[6] Almost a third of all Old Testament quotes in the Pauline Letters are found in Rom. 9–11.

[7] Because so vast a number of articles and books have been written about hermeneutics in general and the argumentation in Romans in particular, the secondary literature for the most part is not dealt with at any great length. The scholarly discussion has to be limited to the more relevant issues only. See, e.g., Hofius 1989b, 175n1: "Die Auseinandersetzung mit anderen Deutungen muß angesichts der umfangreichen Sekundärliteratur und der überaus divergierenden Auffassungen der Exegeten weithin implizit erfolgen." In a similar way, Barrett 1977, 99, writes, "It is unnecessary here to remark on the immense body of literature that this passage, and this theme, have evoked; equally unnecessary, I hope, to point out that a review of this literature, even if I were competent to make it, is out of question." Further,

see the limited scope in the foreword to Hübner 1984, 5. By and large, I agree with his approach to the quite extensive secondary literature: "In der Regel blieben vor allem jene Beiträge unberücksichtigt, in denen Röm 9–11 nicht primär aus exegetischen Gründen behandelt wird, sondern 'nur,' um das Verhältnis Kirche—Judentum neu zu bedenken." In certain cases, there are detailed references in my other publications, especially Laato 1991 and 1995 (also 2004, 343–53; 2008, 40–73). An extensive and excellent survey of the latest research concerning "the New Perspective on Paul" is presented by Westerhom 2004b. Cf. further his other article from that year (2004a, 1–38). Issues such as the very heated debate over the exact meaning of the terms *works* or *works of the law* will be completely passed over below, though it should be said that I certainly do not agree with the New Perspective's position that they stand only for "Jewish identity markers" (circumcision, Sabbath, food regulations, etc.). See Laato 2019, especially 304–6.

II. Hermeneutic Presuppositions

[1] Goppelt 1981b, 262–63. For the German original, see Goppelt 1981a, 31: "'Rein historisch' bedeutet gerade nicht objektive Wissenschaftlichkeit, sondern [. . .] 'eine ganze Weltanschauung' als Denkvoraussetzung. War durch das historisch-kritische Prinzip die Schriftforschung letztlich nur dazu von der kirchlichen Tradition bzw., wie oft gesagt wird, von der Metaphysik befreit worden, um sie desto mehr von der jeweiligen Zeitphilosophie abhängig zu machen? Gibt es einen Ausweg aus diesem Dilemma? Teilen wir nicht unausweichlich die Denkvoraussetzungen unserer Zeit?" See also Wenz 1996, 147: "So bleibt als Fazit: 'Das Sicherste,' was die historische Forschung 'zustandegebracht hat, ist die Tatsache, daß die Identifizierung des wesenhaft Christlichen ein rein historisch nicht lösbares Problem ist.'"

[2] Goppelt 1981b, 25–35.

[3] See Bonhoeffer 1988 and 1996.

[4] See W. Neuer's introduction in the new edition of A. Schlatter's articles concerning hermeneutical questions (Schlatter 2002, 13): "Bei allem zeitgeschichtlichen Kolorit der Ausführungen wird deutlich, dass sich die Grundprobleme biblischer Hermeneutik zu Beginn des 21. Jahrhunderts nicht viel anders darstellen als zu Schlatters Zeit." Further, it is noted that Schlatter's theses "transcend time and deserve attentive study also today" (7, my translation; über seine Zeit hinausweisen und auch heute noch ein aufmerksames Studium verdienen).

[5] Jäger 1905, 577–82. Translations of Jäger and Schlatter below are my own.

[6] Schlatter 1905, 229–50. The article has been published again in the edition that was revised by W. Neuer (Schlatter 2002, 131–48).

[7] The German word *Wissenschaft* literally translates to "science" or "scholarship" but is often used in the sense of "academic discipline."

[8] Jäger 1905, 579: "[. . .] daß die gesamte Wissenschaft bei ihrer Arbeit den Gottesgedanken aus dem Spiele läßt und völlig konsequent die Welt aus der Welt selbst zu erklären unternimmt. Man sollte doch so gerecht sein, zuzugeben, daß in der Tat die Wissenschaft, so wie die Dinge liegen, keine andere Methode haben *kann*."

[9] Schlatter 1905, 239: "Denn sein [sc. Jägers] Weltbegriff, der der Welt die atheistische Verschlossenheit in sich selber gibt, so daß im ganzen Bereich des Geschehens nirgends etwas anderes sichtbar werden darf und kann als die Welt, ist selbst eine Dogmatik, aber eine wertlose Dogmatik, schon deshalb, weil sie nicht erarbeitet und begründet ist."

[10] Jäger 1905, 579: "Denn die Theologie hat nur so lange Gleichberechtigung im Rahmen der *Universitas Litterarum*, als sie aufrichtig und ehrlich und nicht blos zum Schein die allgemein anerkannte wissenschaftliche Methode mit vertreten kann. Kann sie das nicht, so muß sie die Entschlossenheit haben, auszutreten."

[11] Schlatter 1905, 242: "Jedenfalls wäre der atheistische Theologiebetrieb das sicherste Mittel, die theologischen Fakultäten zu zerstören. Wenn es einmal wirklich dahin kommt, daß unsere Studenten das Neue Testament nur so lesen wie Homer, und unsere Exegeten es erklären wie Homer mit entschlossener Ausstoßung jedes auf Gott gerichteten Gedankens, dann ist es mit den theologischen Fakultäten vorbei."

[12] Jäger 1905, 582: "Wenn wir Wissenschaftlichkeit und Frömmigkeit als zwei verschiedene Vergegenwärtigungsarten derselben Inhalte auseinanderhalten, so kann es nicht mehr für ungeheurlich gelten, wenn auch Theologen die religiös indifferente 'historische' oder 'immanente' Methode auf ihrem Gebiete anwenden."

[13] Schlatter 1905, 244: "Nun aber, nachdem auch die Theologie atheistisch geworden ist: woher kommen jetzt noch 'höhere Erkenntnisse'? [. . .] Das letzte, tiefste Wort spreche der Theologe freilich nicht; wer spricht es dann? Jedenfalls nicht das Neue Testament, denn dieses haben wir ja 'ohne Zuhilfenahme des Gottesgedankes erklärt.'"

[14] Schlatter 1905, 248: "Wenn wir nun aber die Religion aus der Welt erklären wollen, so stellen wir uns bei der Beobachtung von Anfang und konsequent in einen radikalen Widerspruch mit unserm Objekt, das eben nicht aus der Welt erklärt sein will, sondern den Gottesgedanken laut und beharrlich geltend macht. Unser Objekt will, daß wir an Gott denken; der Beobachter will 'ohne Hinzunahme des Gottesgedankes' denken. [. . .] Und je mehr wir nicht nur beobachten, sondern erklären wollen, je mehr das Objekt in unser fertiges Schema hineingezwungen werden soll, um so stärker wird die wissenschaftliche Karikatur; um so sicherer verwandelt sich die angebliche Wissenschaft in

Polemik gegen ihr Objekt, und es entsteht der nicht das Geschehene, sondern den Historiker bekundende Roman."

[15] See especially Gruenler 1991, 21–35.

[16] Ibid., 35–45. See further Gardner 1999, 329–42.

[17] The word atheism in current usage means an opinion that denies that there are any gods. However, an atheistic undertone comes into even such contexts where one does not straight away place a big question mark on God's existence but nonetheless already in advance excludes the transcendent. Cf. Harris 1990, xxi–xxii: "The word *a-theistic* (and its cognate *a-theological*) here means the principle which *excludes* the supernatural, without any decision being made as regards the actual existence or non-existence of God, i.e. it is not the same word as *atheistic*, which *denies* the idea of a divine being."

[18] Gruenler 1991, 35–109. See further Bayer 2002. Wenz has written a very clarifying review of the book (2003, 194–99).

[19] Gruenler 1991, 71.

[20] Vanhoozer 1998, especially 37–195. See also Carson 1996, 66–67: "But with Immanuel Kant, there was injected into modernity a seed that would grow and grow and ultimately destroy it. [. . .] But the fact remains that 'in Kant's philosophy, human consciousness begins to be not only the key for discovering reality, but the source of reality itself' [in reference to T. Finger]."

[21] See Vanhoozer 1998, 38. Cf. Carson 1996, 72–77.

[22] Cf., e.g., Vanhoozer 1998, 108: "Most appropriations to date of literary methods by biblical scholars correspond to this conservative version of 'reader-response' criticism. The text has certain indeterminacies or gaps that the reader needs to fill in, but the text itself provides some guidance as to how to do so."

[23] Gruenler 1991, 64–71.

[24] Cf. Hägglund 2011, 59–60. Concerning the presuppositions of theological discipline, it is often postulated that we cannot take for granted, for example, the resurrection of Jesus as the basis of academic research. So then the pushed principle reads that Bible scholarship should merely confine itself to atheistic or agnostic methods, assigning particularly the church the task of preaching. But here a more precise analysis is needed. Strictly speaking, the resurrection of Jesus deals with *special* revelation. The discussions about the "God hypothesis" as an axiomatic starting point of true knowledge draw on the *general* revelation. The distinction between the two aspects should not be ignored. For a more thorough consideration of the hermeneutics in Romans, see chapter 4 below.

[25] Eastman 2017, 10–11.

[26] Ibid., 92 (in reference to D. Martin).

[27] Ibid., 16 (in reference to T. Chappell).

[28] Ibid., 92 (in reference to V. Reddy).

[29] Ibid., especially 6–26.

[30] See, e.g., Karavidopoulos 2000, 160: "In der westlichen biblischen Forschung wurde diese [historisch-kritische] Methode zudem *die* Methode par excellence, obwohl heute nach-strukturalistische Kritik (Reader-response criticism, Dekonstruktion usw.) die historisch-kritische Methode von ihrer zweihundertjährigen Vorherrschaft zu entthronen scheint."

[31] For this, see Keskitalo 2004, 72–89.

[32] Cf. Henttonen 1997, 162ff. He rightly argues (165) that today, scholarly theology often coincides with analytical philosophy of religions: "Onkin melko vaikeaa havaita, mikä erottaa tällaisen [= ateistisen] teologian analyyttisesta uskonnonfilosofiasta. Jos tuota eroa ei enää ole löydettävissä, voitaneen välittömästi esittää kysymys, mihin teologiaa sitten vielä tarvitaan?" (It is quite difficult to figure out what the difference is between the [atheistic] theology and analytical philosophy of religions. If a difference can no longer be found, one may immediately ask the question, what use does theology have anymore?) Cf. further 167.

[33] See, e.g., Marshall (1982, 84–85), who presents a well-balanced assessment of the state of research. Cf. further already Lohfink 1967, 71–75. In a similar way (although in an even more radical form), see Linnemann 1990, 84, 114–23.

[34] It does not help any if, for example, agnostic methods are discussed instead of atheistic ones.

[35] See above. Further, take notice of Dunn's evaluation of the state of the research in his short article (2000, 105–21). Cf. Linnemann 2001, 182–85; Maier 1975, 47–54. In Sweden, see Erlandsson 1971, 132–36.

[36] Etymologically *criticism* simply means "seeking of truth." See Sasse 1981, 233: "Wobei die Bemerkung nicht unterdrückt sei, daß das Wort 'Kritik' im Sinne der historischen Forschung nichts anderes ist als der technische Ausdruck für 'Untersuchung'. Plato, der Vater der abendländischen Wissenschaft, definiert das 'krinein,' das 'Untersuchen' als ein 'sozein ta phainomena,' ein Retten der Phänomene, das heißt die Bemühung, eine Sache dadurch zu verstehen, daß man sie zu ihrem Recht kommen läßt, ihr gerecht wird, indem man ihr tiefstes Wesen versteht." Likewise, see Marshall 1982, 78: "'Criticism' in this case simply means 'study,' and we cannot avoid practising it if we want to find out what any text in the New Testament is saying. Either we do it ourselves, or we get somebody else to do it for us."

[37] See especially Marshall 1982, 92–93. Cf. above.

[38] It is quite symptomatic that the Old Testament exegetes time and again reach completely different results when it comes to dividing the textual material between several imagined redactors. Sometimes I get the impression that a talented professor and his own students (but none other) achieve the same conclusion! See, for example, the treatment of the so-called Deuteronomic

concept of history. Cf. Carson 1986, 8: "But having destroyed all the preten-
sions of external authority, we have discovered, somewhat aghast, that reason
is corruptible, that one human mind does not often agree in great detail with
another human mind."

[39] Given the historical-critical method, Marshall rightly argues, "One must
not condemn all its works out of hand, since undoubtedly much valuable
work has been done by proponents of it, and we would be the poorer without
what has been done" (1982, 85). Later he adds: "It is possible to distinguish
between the proper use of methods of linguistic and historical study and the
adoption of sceptical presuppositions." Even Maier continues to work with
the conventional methods (1975, 80–89) despite the fact that he has presented
his negative view of the historical-critical position. Roberts argues in the same
way (1995, 132): "Though I feel no compulsion to offer a blanket defense of
the historical-critical method as theoretically conceived, much less as it has
been practiced by many different scholars in the field, I am deeply suspicious
of the current tendency to denigrate previous OT scholarship." Furthermore,
cf. Joyce 1994, 20: "The absolute rule of the historical-critical approach, with
its excessive claims and its undermining effect on the functioning of Scripture,
has been ended for good and that is no bad thing. But serious questions remain.
[. . .] Has the historical-critical approach, with all the considerable benefits it
brought, no place? Is the baby to be thrown out with the bathwater?"

[40] Neuer in Schlatter 2002, 13: "Eine nachdrückliche Verteidigung der
reformatorischen Auffassung von der prinzipiellen Klarheit der Schrift ('clari-
tas Scripturae'), welche die vorreformatorische Bindung der Schrifterkenntnis
an die theologisch gebildete Priesterschaft bzw. das kirchliche Lehramt ebenso
bestreitet wie die seit der Aufklärung üblich gewordene protestantische
Neigung, die Schriftauslegung an wissenschaftliche Spezialisten zu binden."
Cf. Carson 1986, 46–48. In the same way, see Roberts 1995, 131 (partly in connection to G. Lindbeck): "It is now the scholarly rather than the hierarchical
clerical elite which holds the Bible captive and makes it inaccessible to ordinary folk." See also especially Joyce 1994, 18n2: "It is ironic that one of the
long-term effects of the Enlightenment was that academic experts came to
replace ecclesiastical authorities as those who exercised the role of arbiter of
the meaning of biblical texts, while the ordinary believer remained in a largely
passive role."

[41] In connection to K. Rahner, Henttonen (1997, 168) even argues that by
discounting God's existence and intervention in history, theological research
commits "suicide": "Olisi vain sääli sitä aikaa, joka käytettäisiin sellaisiin
Jumalan hautajaispuheisiin; positivistinen luonnontieteilijä, jolle Jumala jo
etukäteen on suljettu pois, olisi rehellisempi ja sympaattisempi kuin teologi,
joka julistaa omaa tuhoaan." (It would be a shame to waste time while speaking at God's funeral; a positivistic scientist for whom God is already excluded

from the beginning is more honest and sympathetic than a theologian, who proclaims his own destruction.)

III. Biblical Hermeneutics

[1] Barth 1945, 305ff.

[2] Ibid., 505ff.

[3] Richardson 1966, 79–80, 100–101. See also Jeanrond 1991, 45. He writes cuttingly concerning Barth's hermeneutical program: "Although he named his dogmatics 'Church Dogmatics' and thus pointed to the social context of his theological reflection, he never advanced to theological reflection on the biblical text which was open to a mutually critical relationship with any other tradition or movement. Barth knew what he thought of the world and of all intellectual exercises that were concerned with the world—namely, not much."

[4] Bultmann 1988.

[5] Cf., e.g., Richmond 1978 and Althaus 1958. The former stresses the similarities between Barth and Ritschl, whereas the latter emphasizes the affinities between Bultmann and Ritschl. Before his great breakthrough, Ritschl represented the so-called Tübingen School, which as a whole builds on an atheistic position. See Harris 1990, 101–12. In summary, he states, "This, in fact, was the one presupposition which determined the whole of Baur's historical investigation and also that of the Tübingen School. On this point all the members of the School were agreed. [. . .] *Not the Hegelian philosophy, but the acceptance or rejection of a transcendent personal God determined Baur's dogmatic and historical investigations*" (252), or, "If one had to sum up the aim and object of the Tübingen School in a single statement it would be that the Tübingen School made the first comprehensive and consequent attempt to interpret the New Testament [for more concerning this, see xxi–xxvii] and the history of the early Church from a non-supernatural (indeed, anti-supernatural) and non-miraculous standpoint" (255).

[6] Theologians have generally passed by Bonhoeffer's *Akt und Sein* (originally published 1931) with silence, allegedly on the basis of its incomprehensible content. They have often not even reviewed the book. Cf. H. R. Reuter's revealing foreword to a new edition (1988, 12). He notes that reviews by H. E. Eisenhuth in *TLZ* and H. Knittermeyer in *Zwischen der Zeiten* appeared two years subsequent to publication: "Besprechungen von 'Akt und Sein' erschienen nach zwei Jahren von Heinz Erich Eisenhuth in der 'Theologischen Literaturzeitung' und von Hinrich Knittermeyer in 'Zwischen den Zeiten.'"

[7] Bonhoeffer 1988, 76: "Mit der Kontingenz ist aber die Vernunfttranszendenz behauptet, d. h. absolute Freiheit der Offenbarung gegenüber der Vernunft und damit gegenüber allen aus einer als Potentialität verstandenen Existenz etwa zu entfaltenden Möglichkeiten." In English, Bonhoeffer 1996, 82: "The transcendence

of reason is asserted along with its contingency—that is, the absolute freedom of revelation as opposed to reason and, consequently, to all possibilities that could be developed, for example, from existence understood as potentiality."

   [8] Bonhoeffer 1988 passim. He writes, for example, right at the beginning of his own interpretation of revelation in the following manner: "Vielmehr kann nur aus der geschehenen und geglaubten Offenbarung und ihrer Wahrheit heraus die Unwahrheit des menschlichen Selbstverständnisses durchschaut werden. Wäre es nicht so, so würde die Offenbarung als letztes Postulat menschlichen Denkens in die Unwahrhaftigkeit des Selbstverständnisses selbst hineingezogen, so daß der Mensch aus den Postulaten seiner eigenen Existenz heraus in die Lage gesetzt wäre, sich selbst recht zu geben und in die Wahrheit zu stellen, was doch eben immer nur die Offenbarung, soll sie als solche wirklich gemeint sein, selbst tun kann. Mithin: nur der in Wahrheit Gestellte vermag sich in Wahrheit zu verstehen" (75). In English, Bonhoeffer 1996, 81: "On the contrary, the untruth of human self-understanding is made clear only from within revelation and its truth, once it has taken place and has been believed. Were it not so, revelation would itself be pulled into the untruthfulness of self-understanding as the final postulate of human thought, with the result that human beings would be put in the situation, from the postulates of their own existence, of adjudging themselves right and placing themselves into the truth. But this is something that only revelation can accomplish, if it is truly understood as such. Therefore, only those who have been placed into the truth can understand themselves in truth."

   [9] Bonhoeffer 1988, 135–61 passim. Cf. 87: "Danach ist meine Erkenntnis Gottes je daran gebunden, ob Gott mich in Christus erkannt hat (1. Kor. 13,12; Gal. 4,9)." In English, Bonhoeffer 1996, 92: "Accordingly, my knowledge of God depends in each instance on whether God has known me in Christ (1 Cor. 13:12; Gal. 4:9)."

   [10] On the definition of the concept, see Bonhoeffer 1988, 22–24.

   [11] Bonhoeffer 1996, 122. In German, Bonhoeffer 1988, 119: "Glaube ist in 'bezug auf' Sein (Gemeinde), nur im Glauben erschließt sich, bezw. 'ist' Sein (Gemeinde), dies Sein aber erkennt der Glaube als unabhängig von sich, sich selbst als eine Seinsweise desselben. Sein transzendiert das Seiende, es ist des Seienden wie auch des Ich eigener Seinsgrund. So kommt Akt aus Sein her, wie er auf Sein hingeht. Sein wiederum ist in bezug auf Akt und doch frei. Offenbarungs-Sein als in der Schwebe zwischen Gegenständlichem und Nichtgegenständlichem ist 'Person,' Gottes offenbarte Person, und Persongemeinschaft, die durch sie begründet ist. Hier fügen sich transzendentaler Ansatz vom 'Sein nur im Akt' und die ursprüngliche ontologische Grundthese von der Freiheit des Seins dem Akt gegenüber, vom Aufgehobensein des Akts im Sein unerwartet ineinander." See also 128: "Now this sociological category that we have discovered here proves to be the point of

unity of the transcendental and the ontological approaches to knowledge. The person 'is' only in the act of self-giving. Yet, the person 'is' free from the one to whom it gives itself. It is through the person of Christ that this understanding of person is won; it has validity only for the personal community of the Christian church, which is based in Christ." The German original in 1988, 125: "Nun erweist sich die aufgefundene soziologische Kategorie als Einheitspunkt des transzendentalen und ontologischen Erkenntnisansatzes. Nur im sich gebenden Akt 'ist' Person. Dennoch 'ist' Person frei von dem, dem sie sich gibt. Dieses Personverständnis ist durch die Christusperson gewonnen und gilt nur für die in Christus gründende Persongemeinschaft der christlichen Kirche."

[12] See Bonhoeffer's criticism of earlier theology, 1988, 27–74.

[13] See, for example, ibid., 87, 101.

[14] On Bonhoeffer's modifications of his dissertation, see Reuter's "Nachwort" (1988, 174–85).

[15] See Sasse 1995, especially the editor J. Kloha's analysis of Sasse's view of Scripture (337–423). Similarly, Müller—Herrmann 2010. Cf. Wachler 1984 (he seems not to be aware of Sasse's later reorientation).

[16] Bonhoeffer 1988, 75–99. To only present one enlightening example: "Darum aber ist alles System des Menschen, der nicht ewig in Wahrheit *ist*, unechtes System und muß zerbrochen werden, damit das echte System möglich werde. Dieser Bruch geschieht im Glauben durch die Predigt" (84). The English translation (1996, 89–90): "But that is why any system of human beings, who *are* not eternally in the truth, is an untrue system and must be shattered so that the true system may become possible. This breaking-apart happens in faith through preaching."

[17] Bonhoeffer 1988, 99–104.

[18] Ibid., 101–2.

[19] Carson 1997, 810.

[20] Here I only refer to Laato 1991, 94–184; 1995, 75–146; and 2004, 343–53.

[21] See my discussion in the previous chapter.

[22] Eastman 2017, 9.

[23] Laato 1991, 95; 1995, 75.

[24] Ibid. 1991, 96; 1995, 76.

[25] Eastman 2017, 10, 158–60.

[26] On the structure of Romans, see, e.g., Siegert 1985, 112–14.

[27] As a result of the so-called New Perspective on Paul, there has indeed been much discussion about the "real" meaning of justification by faith as well as whether it constitutes the center of New Testament theology or exactly in what manner it relates to the relationship between Jews and Gentiles. This is not the place to go at length into a detailed investigation. Still, see many of my monographs and articles, especially those published in 1991, 1995, 1997, 2003, 2004, 2008, and 2009b. Despite the ongoing discussion and many different

understandings, I think that at least in Romans, justification by faith *is* the main theme (see 1:16–17). Most scholars agree on that, don't they? Besides, here I try to shed more light on the hermeneutics of Romans. In this regard, justification is one important aspect but not the only one. There are other relevant characteristics to be mentioned (see below).

[28] See below.

[29] Lampe 1989, 301–2.

[30] Ibid., 56–57.

[31] See especially Wilson 1991, 130–31, 139–42.

[32] See van der Minde 1976, 39.

[33] I assume that verses 25–26 are from Paul's pen. Cf. the discussion about text-critical problems in various commentaries. See also especially Carson 2004, 422 (he accedes to I. H. Marshall).

[34] Cf. ibid., 422–23.

[35] See the table in Longenecker 1999, 92–98. He includes only direct quotations, not allusions. Cf. Koch 1986, 21–23.

[36] Luther 1960, 380.

[37] Seifrid 2000, 46–47. See also Barrett 1977, 121.

[38] Seifrid 2000, 47.

[39] Schreiner 1998, 542.

[40] For more concerning Rom. 9:33–10:3, see "9:30–10:21" under "Focus on Rom. 9–11," chapter 4.

[41] Cf. already Jer. 23:6, 33:16, where the Messiah is called "the LORD [. . .] our righteousness."

[42] For more on the connection between the "judicial" and "participatory" categories, see Laato 2004, 343–53.

[43] See, e.g., Hägglund 1963, 163–66, 174–78; Schmidt 1982, 683–722; Seeberg 1913, 606–21.

IV. Paul's Way of Reading Holy Scripture

[1] See commentaries above.

[2] LXX reads ὁ δὲ δίκαιος ἐκ πίστεώς μου ζήσεται in reference to God's faithfulness (and not to man's faith).

[3] Cf., e.g., 4:11, 4:13; 9:30, 10:6.

[4] Regarding the argumentation for v. 17, see first and foremost Nygren 1979, 87–98. In connection to him, see Cranfield 1982, 101–2.

[5] Cf. especially Silva 1993, 641.

[6] Cf. Silva's in-depth discussion (1993, 640–41) and also Schreiner 1998, 74–75. For more concerning the relationship between James and Paul, see Laato 2003.

[7] In general regarding the "promise-fulfillment" scheme, see Hahn 2002, 116–19, 814–15, with a list of older and newer secondary literature. Cf., e.g., Carson 2004, 403–4; Longenecker 1999, xxvi–xxx.

[8] See especially Moo 1986, 196: "We suggest that typology is best viewed as a specific form of the larger 'promise-fulfillment' scheme."

[9] The similarity between Adam and Christ lies in their being the heads of the old and new humankinds, respectively.

[10] The similarity lies in *God's* constant negative attitude against apostasy and different transgressions.

[11] Regarding typological reading in general, especially in contrast to allegorical reading, see, e.g., Goppelt 1939. His work is still a classic standard work; in general, all other works follow it. Concerning this, see Koch 1986, 216n1, even if he (in my opinion, certainly less than convincingly) on several accounts criticizes Goppelt (216–20; as to allegorical reading, see 202–16). Hahn, together with his treatment of the characteristics of typology, gives us a list covering older and newer secondary literature (2002, 119–23, 814–15). For a small addition to the general account of New Testament typology, see Laato 2002, 88. Moo (1986, 195) describes the current situation in research as follows: "In the last thirty years, typology has reemerged, after a period of relative neglect, as one of the most popular ways of explaining the relationship between the Testaments." For the later discussion, see Carson 2004, 404–10.

[12] It is worth pointing out here that the Old Testament canon within Judaism in reality had been established even long before the New Testament era. See especially Ellis 1991, 3–50. Similarly, see Skarsaune 2002, 279–93. Cf. already Michel 1929.

[13] Moo 1986, 204–11. Cf. the demonstrable difference between Pauline and Jewish exegesis: "A vast gulf separates the often fantastic, purely verbal exegeses of the rabbis from the generally sober and clearly contextually oriented interpretations found in the New Testament" (193). See further Carson 2004, 410–12.

[14] Evans 1984, 570: "In order to understand Paul's hermeneutic properly it is necessary to view it against the prophetic hermeneutic of the Old Testament. A study of Romans 9–11 proves to be instructive in this." Cf. Hübner 1984.

[15] Among a number of commentaries, see, e.g., Davies 1977–78, 13; Hofius 1989b, 177–78; Rengstorf 1978, 152–53; Rese 1975, 214–15; Sänger 1986, 102. See further Hahn 1982, 225: "Das 'zuerst den Juden' [. . .] wird somit im Blick auf die Heilsvollendung zu einem 'zuerst den Heiden.'"

[16] Cf. already Rese 1975, 215: "Für Paulus steht mehr auf dem Spiel: Durch den Unglauben der Mehrheit der Juden wird die Frage der Besonderheit der Juden verschärft zur Frage nach der Wahrheit Gottes; es geht um Gott selbst und seine Treue zu seinem Wort." Later, see also Wright 1993, 235: "Modern scholarship has rightly focused on the main subject: the Jews' failure to believe the gospel. But it has not so often been noticed that the reason Paul

is discussing this, and the terms in which he is discussing it, have to do not merely with Israel but with God." After this, the question regarding God's *own* righteousness is thoroughly discussed on 235–36. See especially Piper 1993, 19: "What is at stake *ultimately* in these chapters is not the fate of Israel; that is penultimate. Ultimately God's own trustworthiness is at stake."

[17] Cf. Räisänen 1987, 2914: "Ein apologetischer Unterton ist unüberhörbar; man kann an Kritiker denken, die Paulus vorgeworfen haben, seine liberale Stellung zum Gesetz [z. B. der Galaterbrief], die mit seiner Missionstätigkeit unter den Heiden zusammenhängt, diene doch nur zur immer größeren Abneigung Israels gegen den Glauben an Christus (vgl. Apg 21,21.28)." See further 2936. See also Johnson 1984, 94.

[18] Räisänen 1987, 2893: "Während alle diese Themen [klassische dogmengeschichtliche Probleme] wenigstens in Ansätzen in den betreffenden Kapiteln vorhanden sind, herrscht heute große Einmütigkeit darüber, daß die Behandlung des Problems der *Treue Gottes* in bezug auf seine Verheißungen an Israel das eigentliche Anliegen des Apostels ist." Cf. Rengstorf 1978, 152; Walter 1984, 172–73.

[19] Cf. Seifrid 1985, 5–6. In his analysis of chapters 9–11, he also refers to the Apostolic exposition of Scripture in an entire letter as follows: "Throughout the epistle, the question of the relationship of Paul's gospel to the revelation already given to Jewish nation receives attention" (4). Similarly, see Brandenburger 1985, 1–2. For statistics regarding the occurrence of Old Testament quotes in Rom. 9–11, see Longenecker 1999, xviii, 92–98. Cf. further Hübner 1984, 147–60: "Übersicht über die alttestamentlichen Zitate und Anspielungen in Röm 9–11."

[20] See especially Davies 1977–78, 19–39; Moo 1996, 710, 710n71. Against, see, e.g., Ruether 1974, 95–107. In the dialog between church and synagogue, I personally agree with the following overall assessment: "Wer immer zu Abraham gehört, hat also auch an seiner einzigartigen Würde Anteil, und sie geht ihm niemals und unter gar keinen Umständen verloren, selbst dann nicht, wenn der Zustand des Abgetrenntseins von Gott für ihn eintreten sollte. Insofern schuldet die nichtjüdische Christenheit der Judenschaft auch dann Respekt, wenn sie auf ihrer Ablehnung Jesu besteht und in ihr und durch sie sich religiös oder gesellschaftlich oder so und so isoliert" (Rengstorf 1978, 162). The same idea is also presented by Walter 1984, 193: "Es wäre absurd, diesem Paulus, dem Autor von Röm 9–11, so etwas wie 'Antijudaismus' zu unterschieben—ohnehin natürlich nicht einen bewußten, gezielten Antijudaismus (das wirft wohl niemand dem Paulus vor), aber auch keinen tendenziellen, impliziten, zwar unbeabsichtigten, aber in der Konsequenz doch unausweichlichen Antijudaismus; ich sehe keinerlei Anlaß dafür." In addition, Davies writes, "[It is] the bitter irony of history that this colossus of a man [= Paul], who had he been heeded might have created a climate of mutual respect and even affection between Jews

and Christians, was misinterpreted by both and his theology often used as part of the very scheme of salvation to justify the infliction of suffering on Jews, so that until very recently Paul has been regarded as unspeakable among his own people" (1977-78, 37-38). See further the interesting contribution to the discussion by Wright: "The irony [. . .] is that the late twentieth century, in order to avoid antisemitism, has advocated a position (the non-evangelization of Jews) *which Paul regards precisely as antisemitic* [Wright's emphasis]. The two-covenant position says precisely what Paul here forbids the church to say, namely that Christianity is for non-Jews. To this extent, it actually agrees in form with the German Christian theology of the 1930s" (1993, 253). On the other hand, it is completely exaggerated to imply that "rabbinic training" (*rabbinische Schulung*) is not relevant for understanding Paul's letters. Against, see Siegert 1985, 157-64. Cf. my reasoning below.

[21] See, e.g., Moo 1996, 553. Cf. 11:28, which speaks about the Israelites as enemies "as far as the gospel is concerned" (9:1-3) and as loved "as far as election is concerned" (9:4-5).

[22] See Cranfield 1981, 473: "This half-verse is the sign under which the whole section 9.6-29 stands—in fact, the sign and theme of the whole of chapters 9-11."

[23] Cf., e.g., Aageson 1986, 267-68; Ellis 1978, 218-20. See also Moo 1996, 553-54.

[24] For the link between chapters 8 and 9, see Rese 1988, 208-9: "'Weg von Christus,' das ist das genaue Gegenteil dessen, was in Röm 8 der Grund der Siegesgewißheit war, nämlich, daß nichts Paulus und die Christen scheiden könne von der Liebe Gottes in Christus Jesus." See also Piper 1993, 45: "Therefore, Paul's statement in 9:3 must be taken to mean that he 'could wish' to experience what 8:35-39 said the Christian never would experience: to be separated from the love of God in Christ and left under his eternal (2 Thess 1:9) wrath (Rom 5:9)." Similarly, see Räisänen 1987, 2895: "Die Behandlung der Heilsgewißheit in Röm 8 scheint die Frage nach dem Schicksal Israels hervorzurufen." See further Wagner 2003, 45.

[25] Cf. Theißen 2002, 312. Cf. further Rom. 9:15 with an explicit quotation from Exod. 33.

[26] Paul first expresses himself positively ("speak the truth") and thereafter in the negative ("do not lie"). Then he testifies to his honesty in v. 2. Thereby, he emphasizes the very serious nature of his surprising desire. Cf. Brandenburger's comment (1985, 6): "Auffallend ist, wie breit und intensiv die Beteuerung in V. 1 ausfällt. Erst nach drei Ansätzen scheint Paulus der Sache das genügende Gewicht gegeben zu haben."

[27] Moo 1996, 556n7. A very peculiar situation arises here: Christ and the Spirit, who are to witness *for* Paul, actually speak *against* him and insist on his death sentence.

[28] Cf. Thurén 1994, 167, 209.

[29] See, e.g., Amos, who first takes up the judgment of God in chapters 1–9 but then finally in 9:11–25 the promise concerning restoration. In particular, Evans has developed a fundamental comparison between Paul's understanding of Scripture and the hermeneutic of the prophets in the Old Testament (1984, 560–70). He is close to the research of, particularly, J. A. Sanders.

[30] Cf. Evans 1984, 569: "Of special importance to Paul are Torah, by which he establishes the principles of God's sovereign election, and the prophets, by which he is able to clarify his history."

[31] E.g., Räisänen 1987, 2895. See also Piper 1993, 125.

[32] See Rese 1988, 111–12. He points out another similarity between chapters 3 and 9: "Wie in Röm 3. 4 verbindet sich in Röm 9 mit dem Unglauben Israels die Frage nach der Wahrheit Gottes. Doch in Röm 3 wurde diese Frage zugespitzt auf die Frage nach der Gerechtigkeit Gottes, eine Frage, die Paulus vorläufig in Röm 3. 4, endgültig in Röm 3. 21–6 beantwortet. In Röm 9 tritt hingegen die Frage nach der Wahrheit Gottes als Frage nach der Gültigkeit des Wortes Gottes in Erscheinung."

[33] E.g., Piper 1993, 21, 23–24. See also Moo 1996, 560–61.

[34] Piper 1993, 21–23. See further, e.g., Moo 1996, 560, 562n35. Theißen 2002, 313 sees points *b* and *c* as one. Therefore, he only talks about two "corresponding" parts.

[35] Theißen 2002, 313: "Umrahmt wird diese Aufzählung durch den Hinweis auf die Verwandten des Paulus κατὰ σάρκα und den Messias τὸ κατὰ σάρκα."

[36] Concerning different ways to translate and interpret v. 5, see below.

[37] Michel 1978, 295n18.

[38] The account of Israel's privileges begins with "Stichworten aus Kapitel 8" (Räisänen 1987, 2896)—that is, the keywords in chapter 8, "adoption" and "glory."

[39] Cf. Piper 1993, 31–40. Theißen allows both of the "corresponding" parts (see above) to interpret each other (2002, 313): in that case, "adoption," "law," "glory," and "temple worship," as well as further "covenants" and "promises," correspond to each other (cf. similar endings in the Greek words!).

[40] Thurén 1994, 169.

[41] Kuss 1978, 677. Similarly, see Piper 1993, 42: "Since he [= Paul] did not want merely to coordinate 'the fathers' and 'the Christ' ('*whose* are the fathers *and whose* is Christ') but rather wanted to highlight the climactic character of Christ's coming, he employed a grammatical construction which indeed does have a climactic ring to it ('and *from* whom')."

[42] See commentaries.

[43] Moo 1996, 567.

[44] Thurén 1994, 170. Rom. 9:5 can be compared with Phil. 2:9, which cites an ancient hymn: God has "bestowed on him the name that is above every name" (Kyrios or Yahweh). See also Titus 2:11–14.

[45] See Rese 1988, 212: "Dieser Sachverhalt wird verdeckt, wo man meint, in Röm 9.6 werde zwischen einem empirisch-historischen Israel und einem eschatologischen Israel unterschieden, das eschatologische Israel sei identisch mit der Kirche und ihr gälten jetzt die in Röm 9. 4, 5 aufgeführten Privilegien." Cf. also 213. Similarly, e.g., Moo 1996, 574. Additionally, Johnson is completely right to warn against the rather common "replacement theology"—namely, that the church completely and wholly should have taken the place of Israel: "From Paul's time until the present, the church has tended to view its existence independently of Israel. Whether they be exegetes such as Marcion, Harnack, or Bultmann who think the church should rid itself of the Hebrew Scriptures, or any number of pastors in the local church who see the church as the new Israel, whoever they may be, they have violated the clear claims of Paul's exposition." He later adds, "In Paul's view any church which exists independently of Israel ceases therein to be the church as a part of God's salvation plan and becomes simply another religious society" (1984, 100). See further Jewett 1985, 345. First of all, he refers to Beker 1984, 332: "The Church of the Gentiles is an extension of the promises of God to Israel and not Israel's displacement."

[46] Piper 1993, 48–50. See also Aageson 1986, 268; Grindheim 2005, 141; Rese 1975, 209, 212. Similarly, see Barrett 1977, 100. Against *opinio communis*, see Brandenburger 1985, 10, 16–17.

[47] Commentaries usually overlook the fact that the thesis in v. 6a obviously links to the Christological image of God in v. 5. God's word (the Old Testament) has messianic content from beginning to end. Against, see Rese 1988, 209: "Zwischen Röm 9. 1–5 und *Röm 9. 6* ist wieder (wie schon in Röm 9. 1) 'kein unmittelbarer Übergang zu erkennen.'" He refers here to Michel 1978, 298.

[48] Cf. Aageson's summary: "The reliability of *God's word* to Israel was at stake; and it was to *God's word*, the Scriptures, that Paul turned to argue that it had not failed" (1986, 286).

[49] For the stylization, if not the reformulation, of the Old Testament quotations in Rom. 9–11, see Koch 1986. Cf. the more in-depth analysis below.

[50] Moo 1996, 610. Brandenburg 1985, 15–16 has a different view.

[51] Hübner 1984, 16: "Wenn es geschehen konnte, daß Israel das verheißene Heil verspielt hat, hat dann nicht auch Gott sein Gottsein verspielt? Wenn Gott der Gott Israels ist, wie doch das ganze Alte Testament erweisen will, ist dann nicht gerade Gott als dieser Gott Israels und somit in seinem eigentlichen Tun gescheitert? Ein gescheiterter Gott ist aber kein Gott!"

[52] Hübner 1984, 24: "Gott sagt 'ich' und konstituiert so Israel." Similarly, see Aageson 1986, 269–73. See further Wagner 2003, 78, 84–85. Cf. already Exod. 3:13–14 and Piper's analysis of God's name (1993, 75–89)! The line of thought in Rom. 9–11 is to be understood against that background.

[53] See further Grindheim 2005, 142–45.

[54] Moo 1996, 571. Cf. the expression οὐ μόνον δέ (v. 10), which brings the argumentation forward.

[55] For the meaning of the remnant idea in the Old Testament, see Johnson 1984, 93–94, 96. He speaks of the remnant "as a sign of judgment and as a sign of hope and grace" (96) and continues: "Paul had employed it in the former sense in chap. 9, but that is not his intention here [sc. in 11:6] as evidenced by the juxtaposition of the notion of grace." Also, Theißen 2002, 321 affirms, "In 11,1ff. wird der Rest-Gedanke aus Röm 9 neu bewertet: Aus dem Überrest einer Katastrophe wird die Vorhut der Rettung von ganz Israel." Properly speaking, however, the hope for the future emerges already in chapter 9. See Clements 1980, 106–21. I have dealt with the Old Testament idea of the remnant in my (Finnish) article published in 2013, 290–307.

[56] For the typological exposition of Scripture, see the second point under "General Principles," chapter 4.

[57] See especially Piper 1993, 51–53, 56–58, 67–71. Verse 11 clarifies what the expression οὐκ ἐξ ἔργων in v. 12 involves. God's grace precedes all works and is not based on present or future merits.

[58] Theißen 2002, 322. Cf. Hübner 1984, 45.

[59] Here, in general, the commentators usually point out that a similar use of language appears in both chapters 4 and 9: λογίζεται, ἐπαγγελία, σπέρμα, ἐξ ἔργων. Cf. Aageson 1986, 269. Piper 1993, 69–71 also compares 9:6b–8 with 2:25–29 together with Gal. 3:26–29 and 4:21–31.

[60] Wright 1993, 238. Cf. the Pauline thought with the idea of rebirth in Corpus Johanneum!

[61] Dunn 1988, 520–21, 544.

[62] Cf. Thurén 1994, 173. This is the only place in the New Testament where it says that God hates someone! See Moo 1996, 587n79.

[63] Thus argues, e.g., Hofius 1989b, 179–80n16. In that case, the aorist in v. 13 may be interpreted as an ingressive aorist. Cf. further Wagner 2003, 82.

[64] Furthermore, Theißen maintains the following on account of the quotation from Hosea in vv. 25–26: "Aber aus von Gott nichtgeliebten Menschen können geliebte Menschen werden. Daher zitiert Paulus Hos 2,25: 'Ich will nennen . . . meine Geliebte, die nicht meine Geliebte war.' (Röm 9,25) Ist es ganz ausgeschlossen, dass auch Esau, der Nicht-Geliebte, zum 'Geliebten' wird?" (2002, 323).

[65] The expression ἄρα οὖν means "also ist es unbestreitbar so, daß" (see Hübner 1984, 39).

[66] Aageson 1986, 270–71. See also Moo 1996, 594.

[67] Moo 1996, 593. Cf. Aageson 1986, 271. Moreover, he maintains that the contrast "between the God who loves and the God who hates in 9:13 is thematically parallel to the God who shows mercy and the God who hardens in 9:18." See further Hübner 1984, 40; Piper 1993, 158–59.

[68] Here, I only refer to M. Luther's classic work *De servo arbitrio* (published in English in 2012 as *The Bondage of the Will*). Even now, it is surprisingly fresh and up-to-date from an exegetical, dogmatic, and philosophical perspective. Cf., e.g., Siegert (1985, 144–48), who attempts to defend the position of Erasmus! In contrast, see already Maier 1971, 351–400. Cf. Müller 1964, 75–89.

[69] Johnson 1984, 96: "In the OT the hardening motif normally has a redemptive function. This is true in the most classic case of hardening in the OT: the hardening of Pharaoh's heart." See further especially Piper 1993, 159–81.

[70] See above. Theißen 2002, 322: "Bei dieser 'Spaltung' Israels fällt auf, dass Ismael, Esau und Pharao Israel repräsentieren [. . .]. Paulus redet von seinem Volk, als sei es ein fremdes Volk." Similarly, see Grindheim 2005, 147; Hübner 1984, 45.

[71] Regarding the similarities between v. 19 and Wisd. 12:12, see Hübner 1984, 46–47.

[72] Cf. Wisd. 12:12.

[73] Hübner 1984, 46–48. See also Piper 1993, 185–89 (for the Old Testament and Jewish view of the Creator as a potter, see further 194–99).

[74] The section is very thoroughly discussed, for example, by Hübner 1984, 49–55. Cf. later even 11:7 with thought of *Israel's* hardening—"the rest were hardened"—or v. 17, which speaks about the branches that "were broken off," or v. 25, where a similarly careful formulation appears: "hardening has come [from whom?] upon Israel." See Harrington 1992, 59. Otherwise, see Piper 1993, 211–14 without paying close attention to the caution that the apostle uses when it comes to establishing a doctrine of predestination concerning the individual's eternal and irreversible lot in damnation or Israel's horrible fate as God's hardened people.

[75] See also Räisänen's appealing contribution: "Die Diskrepanz zwischen göttlicher Vorherbestimmung und menschlicher Verantwortlichkeit ist allerdings keine paulinische Eigentümlichkeit. Sie kommt im AT, in Qumran und in den Evangelien (vor allem bei Markus und Johannes) vor. Später ist sie auf unzähligen Seiten im Koran anzutreffen" (1987, 2910).

[76] First and foremost, see Piper 1993, 151–216. See further Moo 1996, 590–91. Cf. Brandenburger 1985, 41: "Daraus ergibt sich: Konstitutiv für die inhaltliche Verwendung der Schrift in Röm 9 ist die im Sinne der paulinischen Rechtfertigungsbotschaft interpretierte Schöpfungstheologie."

[77] Grammatically v. 24 is a relative clause to v. 23. Cf. Schlier 1977, 303: "Sachlich wird der Relativsatz zu einem Hauptsatz." See further Piper 1993, 184–85.

[78] Cf. further Grindheim 2005, 147, 150; Hays 1989, 67.

[79] Regarding the subsequent structure, see Brandenburger 1985, 13; Koch 1986, 279–80.

[80] In vv. 25–26, the apostle replaces the verb "to say" in Hosea 1:1–10 and 2:23 with "to call" because he wants to emphasize the connection with v. 23 in particular and with the preceding reasoning in general (concerning the meaning and importance of the verb "to call," see above). In order to be able to begin with a statement about the call, he even changes the sequence of the sentences. So the quotation is adapted to the context, though the content remains the same. See especially Hübner 1984, 56; Koch 1986, 105, 167, 173. Cf. Aageson 1986, 272.

[81] See various commentaries. Brandenburger gives expression to the common or only prevailing view concerning the relevance of the cited Scripture in Rom. 9:25–26: "Wie auch teilweise in Röm 9 beobachtet werden konnte, entnimmt Paulus der Schrift häufig, was sie, historisch beurteilt, nicht enthält" (1985, 41–42). Immediately thereafter, he refers in n65 to the evidence in Rom. 9:25–26. Cf., however, Thießen's reservation: "Meist bezieht man das Hoseazitat nur auf die Heiden. Nur sie wären dann das Nicht-Volk, das zum Volk Gottes wurde. Theoretisch aber könnte man es *auch* auf die Juden beziehen, dann wären Juden eingeschlossen, die Paulus zuvor mit Ismael, Esau und Mose [lies: Pharao?] wie heidnische Völker [. . .] angesprochen hatte" (2002, 331n31). Differently, see Grindheim 2005, 149.

[82] Thurén 1994, 177. Cf. below.

[83] Regarding Jer. 11:16, see Rengstorf 1978, 154. Cf. Walter 1984, 179. He adds in n19, "Merkwürdigerweise wird die Anknüpfung von Röm 11,17 ff an Jer 11,16 f in der Exegese relativ wenig bedacht, sondern nur eben notiert." Perhaps the answer lies at least partially in the fact that Jer. 11:16f. does not use the same language as Rom. 11:17ff. In place of the branches being broken off, it says that they have been burnt.

[84] In addition, the apostolic reasoning lies in line with certain historical facts: Hosea was of course a prophet in the northern kingdom of Israel that was totally destroyed by the Assyrians in the year 722 BC. The people as such (barring particular individuals) never came back to their land. There was never any rehabilitation of the national unity (the Israel of today is another matter). Of the twelve tribes, only three remained: Judah, Benjamin, and Levi. Together they formed the southern kingdom of Judah, which was taken in the year 587 BC. A portion of them came back after captivity in Babylon. If the prophecies in Hosea 1:10 and 2:23 should have any meaning whatsoever beyond the eschatological perspective, then their application to the engrafted

Gentiles—in accord with Paul's argumentation above—would be a resolution to consider.

[85] See especially Moo's clarifying exegesis (2004, 204n62). Earlier in his magnificent commentary (1996), he had still not arrived at this important aspect.

[86] For the shortening of the Old Testament quotation in vv. 27b–28, see Koch 1986, 82–83.

[87] Thurén 1994, 178.

[88] Perhaps the prophet's distress and angst is connected to the fear that the promise to Abraham and his seed would come to nothing: even if his children and descendants would be as numerous "as the sand of the sea, only a remnant of them will be saved" (see the argumentation above). Has God then betrayed his people? Has he broken his oath? The gospel gives a final answer with its joyous message that the Gentiles, too, shall be counted as children of Abraham by faith.

[89] Aageson 1986, 273. He attaches his attention to a similar use of language in v. 10 and v. 11 ("the Children of the living God" and "the children of Israel"). Besides, Isa. 10:22 speaks about the *people of Israel*, an expression that eventually does not quite fit in the context of Romans, where the Gentiles are addressed as "my people" (cf. 9:25–26, 27–28)! See further Grindheim 2005, 151; Koch 1986, 167–68; Shum 2002, 206–7.

[90] NIV translates v. 28 as "The Lord will carry out his sentence on earth with speed and finality."

[91] Grindheim 2005, 141–42.

[92] Cf. Schlier's interpretation: "Jedenfalls wird in V 28 zum Ausdruck gebracht, daß 'der Herr,' selbst seine Verheißung verkürzend, nur einen 'Rest' retten wollte. Das ist in Erfüllung gegangen, indem Gott tatsächlich sein Wort (sein Heilsgeschehen) eingeschränkt erfüllt hat und so nur ein 'Rest' von Israel seinem letzten Ruf folgte" (1977, 304–5). See further the discussion in Koch 1986, 148–49.

[93] Aageson 1986, 273; Koch 1986, 280.

[94] See Laato 2013, 299–301.

[95] For the significance of the notion of a remnant in Isa. 1:8–9, cf. Clements 1980, 114: "What we have with this development of the remnant theme is not so much a fully rounded 'concept,' or 'idea,' of a remnant, but rather a prophetic catchphrase, or seminal prophecy. Although the original phrase [a reference to Isaiah's son Sear-Jasub; see 7:3] goes back to Isaiah, the roots of the idea which it was used to develop are more loosely to be found in the passage Isa. 1:4–9, where the word 'remnant' is not itself used."

[96] As to political situation in the world during Isaiah's time, see, e.g., Clements 1980, 108–15.

[97] Wright 1993, 245.

[98] Thurén 1994, 179.

[99] Cf. the discussion in Mark 12:28–34 (par.).

[100] Aageson 1986, 274. However, cf. Barrett 1977, 111.

[101] Evans explains the combination of the Old Testament quotations well: "Paul's quotation consists of the opening line of Isa 28,16, a fragment of Isa 8,14, and the last line of 28,16" (1984, 565). Cf. Koch 1986, 59.

[102] Thurén 1994, 180. Cf. further Barrett 1977, 111; Evans 1984, 563; Hübner 1984, 66; Koch 1986, 69, 161; Müller 1964, 33–38.

[103] Against, see proponents for the so-called New Perspective.

[104] See especially Laato 1991, 249–54 (in English: 1995, 197–201). Similarly, see Shum 2002, 217–18, 230 (in reference to Laato).

[105] Schreiner 1998, 542; Wagner 2003, 155–57. See further Laato 2015, 722; above "(3) God's Righteousness—Christ Himself" under "The Hermeneutics of Romans" in chapter 3.

[106] For the discussion, see, e.g., Jewett 1985, 349–54.

[107] See Flückiger 1955, 154: "Grundsätzlich ist jedenfalls zu sagen, daß im biblischen Griechisch an jenen Stellen, wo τέλος mit 'Ende' übersetzt werden kann, die Grundbedeutung 'Ziel' noch mitklingt." Similarly, see Moo 1996, 641n44: "But I am not arguing for a 'double meaning' for the word [= τέλος i v. 4]; I am arguing that the *single* meaning of the Greek word here combines nuances of the English words 'end' and 'goal.'" See also Barrett 1977, 115: "It must be recognized that these terms [different alternatives to translate v. 4] are by no means mutually exclusive. When an instrument has been used to achieve its intended goal it may well, without disparagement, be discarded as no longer useful; and with God object and result are bound to be ultimately identical, since it is unthinkable that he should fail to achieve his goal." See further Seifrid 1985, 7–10. Cf. Theißen 2002, 316. He speaks about "eine gewisse Doppeldeutigkeit" and translates τέλος with "Endpunkt." See Jewett 1985, 353–54.

[108] Especially Badenas (1985) strongly argues for the meaning "goal." Without delving further into his argumentation here, I will only refer to some critical viewpoints, for example, in Schreiner 1998, 544–46 (cf. also below). See further Hofius 1989a, 110–11n217. *Pace* Wagner 2003, 157–65.

[109] Regarding statistics, see Moo 1996, 639n41. Cf. Flückiger 1955, 153–54.

[110] Murray 1982, vol. 2, 50. See further Walter 1984, 178n16; Watson 2004, 332–33.

[111] Moo 1996, 640 and already 623n33.

[112] Murray 1982, vol. 2, 50. See further Nygren 1979, 382: "Ordet om lagens 'telos' gäller endast för dem som genom tron på Kristus fått del av gudsrättfärdigheten. Eljest och utanför trons område härskar lagen."

[113] See already Sanday—Headlam 1920, 265. In reference to him, see Cranfield 1981, 515. Similarly, see Murray 1982, vol. 2, 49–50. Cf. Seifrid 1985, 8.

[114] Murray 1982, vol. 2, 49–50. See further Sanday—Headlam 1920, 265; Seifrid 1985, 8.

[115] The phrases "apart from the law" (3:21) and "the end of the law" (10:4) clearly make a pair of terms. Similarly, "righteousness of God" (3:21) and "Christ" (10:4) seem to be in a relationship to each other, which further confirms the earlier conclusion that Christ in his own person represents God's righteousness.

[116] Especially, Moo (1996, 640n42) has in brief drawn attention to a comparison between 3:20–22 and 10:3–4. See also, e.g., Nygren 1979, 381.

[117] Ibid.

[118] Cf. Berger 1990, 204–5: "Als Luther Röm 10,4a im Deutschen mit 'Ende des Gesetzes' wiedergab, hatte das Wort 'Ende' noch bemerkenswert andere Bedeutungsinhalte als jetzt. So fragte man früher: 'Zu welchem Ende tust du das?' und meinte damit: Mit welchem Ziel, mit welcher Absicht, welches ist das, was am Ende stehen soll?" A real, relevant comment indeed! Cf. the language in 9:30–32, which has some resemblances to the ancient genre of sport (athletics). Moo 1996, 641: "a race course (which many scholars think *telos* is meant to convey)." See further already Barrett 1977, 106; Flückiger 1955, 154–55; Theißen 2002, 317n9, point 2 (with reference also to 9:16 and 11:11). The completion is ended when the goal has been reached!

[119] Laato 2008, 51–52. According to Moo (1996, 642), v. 4 functions as if it were "the hinge on which the entire section 9:30–10:13 turns." Cf. further Seifrid 1985, 15: "The rejection of the pursuit of the law by works is precisely the issue dealt with in 9:30–33. Rom 10:4–10 is basically a restatement and expansion of Paul's earlier proposition."

[120] Schreiner 1998, 550–51.

[121] See Moo 1996, 644: "This theological 'law'/'gospel' antithesis is at the heart of this paragraph [...]. Significantly, Paul finds this distinction in OT itself." Cf. further the contrast between "to do" and "to believe" in the whole pericope.

[122] Ibid., 645n5.

[123] Thurén 1994, 185. Van der Minde (1976, 109) discusses the modification of the Old Testament quotation in Rom. 10:5 but on the basis of an outdated edition of Nestle-Aland. Cf. also Hübner 1984, 79–80, 94. For text-critical remarks on v. 5, see Lindemann 1982, 232–37.

[124] Seifrid 1985, 11–12. Cf. also Jub. 22:14, 32:19. Otherwise, see Lindemann 1982, 241–42.

[125] Seifrid 1985, 12: "Since Leviticus does not envision the sacrifices as absolutely efficacious, it is unlikely that Lev 18:5 refers to making sacrifice as a means of maintaining life."

[126] Ibid., 11n41.

[127] See further Laato 2004, 353–59. In addition, Leviticus prophecies that on account of Israel's grave sins, God will no longer smell the aroma of her

sacrifices "with delight." In that case, the temple cult will cease to have any meaning at all.

[128] Cf. Schreiner 1998, 555–56.

[129] See especially Käsemann 1980, 274–75. In reference to him, Lühking 1986, 209, 209n532. See further, e.g., Thurén 1994, 185. Cf. Koch 1986, 131n50. *Pace* Theißen 2002, 325.

[130] See also Laato 2008, 57. Cf. Moo 1996, 650: "By attributing to the righteousness based on faith the ability to 'speak,' Paul follows the biblical pattern of personifying activities and concepts that are closely related to God." In footnote 24, he refers in particular to the concepts of "Wisdom" and "Word."

[131] Hays 1989, 81; Koch 1986, 185–86, 185–86n78; Seifrid 1985, 36.

[132] See, e.g., Longenecker 1999, 104–6 (partly in reference to Sanday—Headlam 1920, 289). Cf. further Hübner 1984, 86–90.

[133] Schreiner 1998, 556. It is with undoubted intention that Paul reproduces Deut. 30:12–14 in shortened form. He leaves out the phrases "so that we may follow it" (vv. 12–13 CSB) and "so that you may follow it" (v. 14 CSB), which certainly do not quite fit together with a Christological interpretation. Cf. Wilckens 1980, 225. See further Koch 1986, 130–32, 185, 295; van der Minde 1976, 111–12; Theißen 2002, 333. Cf. also Seifrid 1985, 18: "The alteration that Paul makes to the text of Deut 30:11–14 has been overstated." The Israelites themselves (to say nothing of the Gentiles) have not been able to keep the law. So someone else must keep it for them as well as acquire what they lack for their disobedience. Christ has done this. He perfectly fulfills the admonition in Deut. 30:12–14. (See my interpretation below.)

[134] See Hübner 1984, 87: "Das eigentliche Problem ist vielmehr, daß Paulus Worte des Mose gegen das Mose-Zitat in V. 5 stellt und dies ausgerechnet Worte sind, deren Subjekt in Dt das Gebot des Gesetzes ist." See also 85. Barrett maintains that the argumentation in Rom. 10:5–8 "is at best paradoxical, and may well be thought unjustifiable." Then he asks, "In other words, Deut. 30 is saying the same as Lev. 18. Is Paul's exegesis honest? Is it sensible?" (1977, 117).

[135] Cf. Seifrid 1985, 35–36. See also Schreiner 1998, 557–58. Wright argues for the hypothesis of "ongoing exile" (see especially 2013, 139–63). For sure, his reasoning lacks evidence. It is backed up by no noteworthy biblical data. Neither does it do justice to the other Jewish texts. See Laato 2019, 308–16.

[136] Hence Paul is not actually "rewriting Deuteronomy" (*pace* Watson 2004, 340). Cf. Wright 1993, 245: "The 'doing of Torah,' spoken of by Leviticus, is actually fulfilled, according to Deuteronomy, when anyone, be they Jew or Gentile, hears the gospel of Christ and believes it. Each of the three verses in Deuteronomy quoted here [sc. Rom. 10:6–8] end with the phrase 'so that you may do it'; *this*, Paul is asserting, is the true 'doing' of the Torah, of which Leviticus speaks."

[137] In v. 6, it is not about the Ascension of Christ. Cf. Seifrid 1985, 26: "The pattern of incarnation-resurrection is followed elsewhere in the NT (e.g., Phil 2:6–11; 1 Tim 3:16; perhaps 2 Cor 8:9)."

[138] The Pauline phrase "that is" (vv. 6–7) hardly corresponds to *pesher* in Qumran. Moo 1996, 654n40: "The Greek phrase τοῦτ᾽ ἔστιν is widely used in the LXX, Philo, and the NT to introduce an explanation; there is little reason to think that it deliberately echoes the DSS *piśrô*." See already Seifrid 1985, 27–34. Cf. Aageson 1986, 275–76. For the relationship between Bar. 3:29–30 and Rom. 10:6–8, see further especially Seifrid 1985, 20–23. He also discusses translations of Deut. 30:12–14 in the later targums (23–25). Similarly, see Koch 1986, 156–57, 158–60.

[139] Schreiner 1998, 558n16.

[140] Ibid., 559. Here I would like to compromise between Käsemann and Seifrid 1985, 26–27.

[141] Thurén 1994, 184. See also Hays 1989, 81; Wagner 2003, 167. Cf. Cranfield 1981, 541.

[142] See commentaries. Cf. Aageson 1986, 276; van der Minde 1976, 114–18.

[143] Cranfield 1981, 527, 530; see especially Legarth 2004, 85–100. For the conviction that "Jesus is Lord," see further, e.g., 1 Cor. 12:3, 16:22 (cf. Rev. 22:20), Phil. 2:9–11.

[144] Dunn 1988, 609.

[145] Shum 2002, 220–21. Cf. Koch 1986, 133. Or perhaps, already here, Paul has had in mind the word of promise "who calls on the name of the LORD shall be saved" (Joel 2:32) that is later cited in v. 13 (Aageson 1986, 276; cf. Wagner 2003, 169).

[146] Schreiner 1998, 561.

[147] Dunn 1988, 609.

[148] Koch 1986, 133–34.

[149] Aageson 1986, 276; Koch 1986, 134.

[150] In general, the commentaries hardly take notice at all of the connection between the context of Joel 2:32 and the argumentation of Romans.

[151] Aageson 1986, 276.

[152] See especially Dunn 1988, 618–20, 627. He discusses vv. 14–21 in context and formulates the rubrics for the whole pericope: "Israel's Failure to Respond to the Gospel" (618). See further Schreiner 1998, 565–72.

[153] Koch 1986, 113–14.

[154] Hübner 1984, 96.

[155] Cf. Lübking 1986, 89: "Bleibt Israels Ungehorsam in V. 14f mehr indirekt im Blickfeld, so wird er in V. 16 unmittelbar angesprochen." See below.

[156] See especially Jeremias 1977, 194–95. See also Theißen 2002, 326n24. Certainly, he immediately thereafter mentions another alternative: "Es [sc. expression 'not all'] könnte sich aber auf alle Hörer des Evangeliums

beziehen, auf Juden und Heiden." Cf. my own interpretation below. See further Hübner 1984, 95.

[157] Dunn 1988, 622–23; Schreiner 1998, 571. Cf. Barrett 1977, 115.

[158] E.g., Thurén 1994, 192. The Rabbis use the word שְׁמוּעָה to mean, in a sense, "doctrine."

[159] Lübking (1986, 90) attempts to show—however, without success—that v. 17 should be a later addition (glossa).

[160] See various translations and commentaries.

[161] Cf. Aageson 1986, 277–78.

[162] See also, e.g., 2 Cor. 4:5–6. The verses speak about faith's origin through the apostolic preaching that has its source in Christ's word and that is further identified with God's creative word (Gen. 1:3). For more about the origin of faith in the Pauline Letters, see Laato 1991, 190–94 (in English: 1995, 150–54).

[163] Murray 1982, vol. 2, 61–62; Schreiner 1998, 571–72. Cf. also Wilcock 2002, 71–73. In a similar way, Hirsch 1978, 134, argues, "[Psalm 19] has as its theme the sources from which one could come to recognize the Lord and worship Him. To David these sources are the book of nature [general revelation], from which he derives his knowledge of God, and the Torah [special revelation], from which he has learned how to worship Him." Later, he continues: "Psalm 19 ends with the hope that this concept of God's dual revelation in nature and in law [. . .] may find favor in the eyes of the Lord."

[164] Cf. Laato 1991, 191–94, 199–204. (In English: 1995, 151–54, 158–62.)

[165] Käsemann 1980, 283–84; Lübking 1986, 91; Schlier 1977, 319; Wilckens 1980, 230. Cf. Moo 1996, 667.

[166] Cranfield 1981, 537–38. See also the discussion in, e.g., Morris 1988, 393.

[167] Cf. Käsemann 1980, 284, concerning the concept of οἰκουμένη: "Bezeichnet wird damit die Ordnung der bewohnten Erde." Similarly, see Schlier 1977, 318.

[168] Cf. also Räisänen 1987, 2908: "Doch wenn die Juden sowohl vor Vers 18 (V. 16!) als auch nach ihm (V. 19:Ἰσραήλ) anvisiert sind, dann muß von ihnen auch V. 18 die Rede sein. Es ist auch nicht einzusehen, welchen Grund Paulus haben könnte, zu betonen, daß die Heiden die Botschaft wohl gehört, aber nicht immer angenommen haben. Das Problem des Paulus ist Israels Unglaube: mit jenem Problem setzt er sich auch in V. 16–18 auseinander."

[169] Thurén 1994, 193.

[170] Cranfield 1981, 538.

[171] See Laato 1991, 252; 1995, 199 (certainly with consideration of the fact that God's own people have rejected God's righteousness, see v. 3). Cf. Cranfield 1981, 538. He fastens his attention to Paul's use of language when he uses the concept Israel (instead of, e.g., the Jews) so pervasively in chapters

9–11, "no doubt because in them he is particularly concerned with the Jewish people as the object of God's election."

[172] Cranfield 1981, 539.

[173] Cf., e.g., Dunn 1988, 625: "The implication [is] that Israel's present lack of 'faith' is the eschatological equivalent of Israel's unfaith in its most idolatrous periods."

[174] Moo 1996, 668n43: "Paul probably introduces this change himself, in order to highlight the 'personal' way in which God [. . .] addresses his people." Cf. Hübner 1984, 97.

[175] Dunn 1988, 520–21, 625.

[176] Schreiner 1998, 574. Cf. Thurén 1994, 194.

[177] Moo argues that the first alternative (= "to a people who did not call on my name") seems to be "the majority view among OT commentators" (1996, 669n49). For occasional exceptions, see ibid.

[178] Cf. Shum 2002, 228–29. He suggests that "the *larger literary context* of Isa.65:1 offers clues in light of which the passage may be understood as speaking of the Gentiles" (229). He refers to J. A. Motyer, who observes thematic parallels between Isa. 65 and 66. They present themselves in a chiastic pattern as follows (see 228):

A   The Lord's call to those who had not previously sought or known him (65:1),

B   The Lord's requital on those who have rebelled and followed cults (2–7),

C   A preserved remnant, his servants, who will inherit his land (8–10),

D   Those who forsake the Lord and follow cults are destined for slaughter because they did not answer but chose what did not please him (11–12),

E   Joys for the Lord's servants in the new creation. The new Jerusalem and its people (13–25),

D′   Those who have chosen their own way and their improper worship. They are under judgment because the Lord called and they did not answer but chose what did not please him (66:1–4),

C′   The glorious future of those who tremble at the Lord's word, the miracle children of Zion, the Lord's servant (5–14),

B′   Judgment on those who follow cults (15–17),

A   The Lord's call to those who have not previously heard (18–21).

Conclusion: Jerusalem is the pilgrimage center of the whole world (22–24).

Finally, Shum concludes, "In sum, viewed from the wider context of Isa.65:1–2 and the entire Isaianic tradition concerning the nations, Paul's use of Isa.65:1 to the Gentiles does seem to make some sense" (229). *Pace* Wagner 2003, 205–16.

[179] Koch 1986, 281.

[180] Barrett is inclined to believe that the sentence "All day long I have held out my hands" (10:21) "may well mean through the whole of Old Testament history" (1977, 106).

[181] Thurén 1994, 195.

[182] Especially Theißen has particularly analyzed the similarities between the life of Paul and the fate of Israel. He summarily draws the following conclusion: "Die persönlichen Einleitungen in Röm 9–11 folgen einer gewissen biographischen Ordnung: Wir hören nacheinander etwas von dem geborenen (9,1ff.) und dem ungläubigen 'Saulus' (10,1ff.), dann von dem erwählten (11,1ff.) und missionierenden 'Paulus' (11,13)" (2002, 320; cf. 317, 331, 335, 337, 339).

[183] Here as well, Theißen maintains a strong "psychological" interpretation that sounds interesting: "Seine [sc. des Paulus] Botschaft ist für die Juden eine willkommene Freudenbotschaft. Wenn sie abgelehnt wird, so hindert das Gott nicht daran, sich trotzdem Israel zuzuwenden. Eben das vollzieht Paulus nach: Wenn er nach Jerusalem reist, so ist seine Reise das Ausstrecken der Hand Gottes nach seinem Volk" (2002, 328).

[184] Lübking 1986, 102: "Der Rest ist nicht wie in 9,27ff Verdeutlichung des Gerichts über Israel, sondern Merkmal der bleibenden Gnade." Similarly, see Moo 1996, 671–72, 679.

[185] Besides, this is how the verb ἐγκατέλιπεν appears in LXX Ps. 93:14b (τὴν κληρονομίαν αὐτοῦ οὐκ ἐγκαταλείψει) as well as in Rom. 9:29 (cf. 11:4).

[186] The commentators often overlook the fact that the historical situation in 1 Sam. 12 (and Ps. 94) is similar to the realities of world politics in Paul's day. However, see already Wright 1993, 247n39: "We should not miss the deliberate 'echo' in 11.2 of 1. Sam. 12.22, in which another Saul, from the tribe of Benjamin, was in himself the evidence that 'God had not forsaken his people.'" Strictly speaking, it is not Saul that becomes a sign that the Lord has not forsaken his people in Samuel's farewell speech. Rather, his designation as king demonstrates Israel's *apostasy*. So v. 25 prophecies that "if you still do wickedly, you shall be swept away, both you and your king" (1 Sam. 12:25). Later, the prophecy is fulfilled with certain penalties (also during the first century AD). First Samuel 12:22 promises a bright future for Israel on the basis of the Lord's "great name's sake." He shall reign over them even if they have rejected him as their king (see 1 Sam. 8). Now Israel has once again rejected the Lord (according to 9:5, the Messiah, Christ!) as their king, but the same promise still applies to them.

[187] Verse 8:29 talks about the *individual's* election. But 11:2 apparently points to the election of the *people* of Israel in accordance with the usual Old Testament and Jewish understanding.

[188] See Moo 1996, 673: "Despite her disobedience, Israel remains 'the people of God'—in what sense, Paul will explain in the rest of the chapter."

[189] Cf. the phrase/expression ἐν'Ηλίᾳ/ with Mark 12:26.

[190] However, cf. the sharp observation of Theißen 2002, 335: "Elia ist ein Beispiel für 'Eifer.' [...] Denn mochte sich Paulus auch früher als ein Eiferer nach dem Modell des Elia und des Pinehas verstanden haben, so tut er es jetzt nicht mehr. [...] Deswegen lässt er in der Klage des Elia in 3 Rg 19,10 LXX [1 Kings 19:18] das Motiv des Eifers aus." See also 318–19n13. Cf. Barrett 1977, 114: "It is worth noting that Paul as a Christian does not speak of having ζῆλος Θεοῦ."

[191] For the two Old Testament quotations in vv. 3–4 in comparison with the original text, see Koch 1986, 74–77. He thinks, "Es handelt sich jeweils um Verbesserungen des z. T. äußerst ungeschickten Übersetzungsgriechisch an diesen beiden Stellen" (76). He adds later, "Paulinische Herkunft ist für die Überarbeitung dieser beiden Zitate nicht wahrscheinlich zu machen." Also, take note that the feminine article comes before the masculine subject Baal! In accordance with the Jewish use of language, in such a case, one ought to read αἰσχύνη ("shame") in the place of the idol's name (Thurén 1994, 196). At least Jer. 3:24 as well as Hosea 9:10 speak of Baal as "the shameful thing" and "the thing of shame," respectively.

[192] Cf. Moo 1996, 677: "It is possible that Paul also finds a parallel between Elijah and himself: each is a key salvation-historical figure, is confronted with the apparent downfall of spiritual Israel, but finds new hope in God's preservation of a remnant of true believers." For a more detailed discussion on the (typological) similarities between Elijah and Paul, see Theißen 2002, 318–20. In another context, he maintains: "So wie Elia offenbart wurde, dass weit mehr als er allein Gott treu geblieben sind, so erhält Paulus die Offenbarung: Nicht nur ein Rest, sondern ganz Israel wird gerettet werden" (336). Cf. also Johnson 1984, 95. *Pace* Lübking 1986, 101. Cf. Müller 1964, 45.

[193] Thurén 1994, 197.

[194] See Hübner's comparison of the argumentation in chapters 9 and 11 (1984, 103).

[195] Aageson 1986, 282; Lübking 1986, 103.

[196] As to the possible reason for the adjustment of the text, see Theißen: "Paulus betont noch entschiedener den vorübergehenden Charakter dieses Unverständnisses [der Juden], indem er das Herz, ein konstantes Organ, gegen einen vorübergehenden Zustand, den Geist der Betäubung (aus Jes 29,10), eintauscht" (2002, 327; cf. 336). See also Shum 2002, 234–35. *Pace* Hübner 1984, 104. In contrast, Koch 1986, 171, speaks about "eine Verschärfung der Verstockungsaussage."

[197] Moo 1996, 681–82; Shum 2002, 232. Notice that Paul attributes the motive of hardening to God (rather than the Lord). Apparently he attempts

to avoid "ein mögliches Mißverständnis vom κύριος im Sinne von Χριστός" (Koch 1986, 121; see also 87).

[198] For those minor changes, see Evans 1984, 567; Wagner 2003, 257–65.

[199] Aageson 1986, 282.

[200] Evans 1984, 568n25. Cf. already the Old Testament passages, such as Deut. 29:4; Isa. 42:18–19; Jer. 5:21; Ezek. 12:2.

[201] Cranfield 1981, 552.

[202] Koch 1986, 138, 138n30; Käsemann 1980, 289; Wilckens 1980, 239. See also Dunn 1988, 650.

[203] Michel 1978, 342. See also Dunn 1988, 650.

[204] Thurén 1994, 198.

[205] Ibid., 211.

[206] Hübner 1984, 107, concludes, "Erst auf dem Hintergrund der durch Gott gewirkten Verblendung *als* Heilswirkung für die Heiden wird der gegenwärtige Zustand Israels 'erklärlich.'" See already 9:17 above.

[207] Moo 1996, 671, 686. Cf. Lübking 1986, 103, 108.

[208] Moo 1996, 685n4. Cf. Lübking 1986, 112, 117–18.

[209] Cf. Theißen 2002, 321: "In Röm 11,11ff. wird der Eifersuchtsgedanke aus Röm 10 neu interpretiert. Aus der aggressiven Ablehnung [Röm. 10:2] wird eine nachahmende Konkurrenz von Juden und Christen auf dem Weg zum gleichen Ziel."

[210] However, it is not necessarily a case of anti-Semitism. See above section "(1) Prologue."

[211] Cf., e.g., Johnson 1984, 99: "It is instructive to consider which metaphor Paul does not use. One might have expected one in which God cuts down the unfruitful tree and plants in its place a completely different tree. That is precisely the concept Paul tries so intensely to expunge from the church."

[212] Aageson 1986, 282–84.

[213] Plag tries to convince readers that Rom. 11:25–27 should be considered "Überrest eines anderen Paulusbriefs" (1969, 65; see further 41, 66). But see Hvalvik 1990, 88–89: "But there are a lot of weighty arguments against Plag's hypothesis. It is, therefore, no surprise that he has met with little, if any, approval from other scholars."

[214] Verse 26a should not be translated as "and in the following way, all Israel will be saved as it is written," in concert with Stuhlmacher 1971, 560. Against his interpretation, see, e.g., Räisänen 1987, 2918–19n154; Sänger 1986, 107–8. Neither is the particle οὕτως (v. 26a) any real designation of time. Rather, it points to the manner in which Israel will be saved—namely, in accordance with that process of salvation outlined in vv. 11–24 and summarized in v. 25. Nevertheless, there is a temporal aspect included in the expression "for the manner in which all Israel is saved involves a process that unfolds in definite stages" (Moo 1996, 720). Similarly, see Grindheim 2005, 167–68n115;

Lübking 1986, 123. Take notice also of Hahn 1982, 227; Hofius 1989b, 192–93; Hübner 1984, 110; Hvalvik 1990, 96–97; Jeremias 1977, 198–99. For similarities between Rom. 11:26a and Isa. 45:25, see Hofius 1989b, 202; Hübner 1984, 113.

[215] Moo 1996, 712.

[216] See, e.g., Sänger 1986, 107, 115. The concept of "mystery" first appears in Daniel (2:17–18, 2:27–30, 2:47). Even the mystery religions of antiquity spoke about different mysteries. But Paul does not link to them. His use of language is derived from the Old Testament or Judaism (see, e.g., Harrington 1992, 58). In the Pauline Letters, the concept of "mystery" normally refers to the gospel (*passim*) but in Rom. 11:25 and 1 Cor. 15:51, to a course of events before or in connection with the end of world history. See Sänger 1986, 112–14. However, he surprisingly does not think that vv. 25–26a present any new thing or any "mystery" in light of what was said previously (108–12). Cf. further Johnson 1984, 101. In contrast, see Moo 1996, 716–19.

[217] Cf. Hofius 1989b, 200–202; see especially Kim 2002, 239–57. Similarly, see Carson 2004, 421–22; Hübner 1984, 121. Jeremias goes even so far as to determine exactly which text in the Old Testament has disclosed the mystery in Rom. 11:25–26 for Paul! He maintains, "Es spricht in der Tat alles dafür, dass es das Wort vom 'Eifersüchtigmachen auf ein Nicht-Volk' (Dtn 32, 21 vgl. Röm 10, 19; 11, 11. 14) gewesen ist, das dem Apostel die Augen für Gottes Pläne mit seinem Volk geöffnet und ihm das Rätsel der Verstockung Israels gelöst hat" (1977, 201).

[218] Against, see first and foremost Jeremias 1977, 199–200. In reference to him, see Ponsot 1982, 406–17—despite his patristic perspective, which F. Javier Caubet-Iturbe formulated as follows: "L'interprétation, depuis le IIIe siècle jusqu'à la fin du XIIe, à l'exception de trois ou quatre commentateurs des IVe et Ve siècles, parmi lesquels il faut compter saint Augustin à certaines époques, a toujours et uniquement compris dans le mot Israël le peuple juif, descendant d'Abraham selon la chair" (quoted in Ponsot 1982, 407). See further Wright 1993, 250. For criticism, see Longenecker 1989, 97. Similarly, see, e.g., Hahn 1982, 221; Räisänen 1987, 2916–17n145. Hvalvik concludes the state of research unequivocally: "As to the meaning of 'all Israel,' there is today almost general agreement that 'Israel' here refers to the Jewish people" (1990, 100). See also Grindheim 2005, 166n113. Cf. Carson 2004, 421, 421n76; Harrington 1992, 59–60.

[219] Grindheim 2005, 166–67.

[220] Harrington lifts up a well-known parallel in the (late) Rabbinic literature: "Mishnah *Sanhedrin*, chapter 10, begins with a general statement: 'All Israel has a portion in the world to come.' Then it proceeds to present a long list of those who have no share in the world to come" (1992, 60). Similarly, see Jeremias 1977, 199: "Das Erstaunliche an diesem Text ist die grandiose

Unbekümmertheit, mit der eingangs ohne jede Einschränkung der Satz auf-
gestellt und durch Schriftbeweis untermauert wird: 'Ganz Israel hat Anteil
an der künftigen Welt' und dann trotzdem eine lange Liste von Ausnahmen
folgt, die in dem (freilich nicht unbestrittenen) Ausschluß der gesamten zehn
Stämme Israels gipfelt." See further Hvalvik 1990, 100. Cf. Müller 1964, 44.

[221] Thurén 1994, 203–4. Hahn 2002, 229, sees it a little differently.

[222] See Moo 1996, 723. Cf. also Grindheim 2005, 167n114. The prophetic
utterance of Jesus in Luke 21:24b corresponds to Rom. 11:25b–26a. He speaks
about Jerusalem's devastation "until the times of the Gentiles are fulfilled"
and uses similar language (cf. the expression ἄχρι and the verb πληροῦν). Cf.
Hübner 1984, 111, in reference to Lagrange: "La conversion des gentils n'est
pas seulement le signal que l'heure est venue: elle aura aussi sans dout *sa part
de causalite* sur celle des Juif." See further Moo 1996, 719.

[223] Here, Longenecker speaks of Paul's "return to a Jewish ethnocentrism"
(1989, 97) in line with the Old Testament: "Although he [Paul] can sustain the
logic of salvation by faith throughout most of Rom. 9–11, at this point [Rom.
11.26] he admits to a salvation which will ultimately spring from an ethnic
condition" (97–98). See also 104, 112–14.

[224] Schreiner 1998, 491: "In addition, 9:6a constitutes the theme of all of
9:6b–11:32, reaching its climax, as already intimated, in 11:26–29, where the
covenantal promise effects the eschatological salvation of Israel. The unbelief of Israel does not nullify God's promises, because nothing can thwart his
word; what he has promised will certainly come to pass." See also Piper 1993,
217–18.

[225] According to certain prominent scholars, the Jews and Gentiles would
each have their own salvation ("bi-covenantal theology," "Zwei Häuser-
Theorie" resp. "Sonderweg"). See, e.g., Mußner 1977, 43–44; Stendahl 1976, 4.
Correctly against that kind of interpretation, see Gräßer 1981, 411–29.
Similarly, see Sanders 1983, 193–95. See also Davies 1977–78, 28; Grindheim
2005, 167n114; Hahn 1982, 230; Hübner 1984, 116–20; Hvalvik 1990, especially
87–91; Jewett 1985, 344; Johnson 1984, 101–2; Longenecker 1989, 99–100;
Lübking 1986, 125–28; Ponsot 1982, 408–9; Räisänen 1987, 2917–18; Sänger
1986, 116–18; Wright 1993, 253–55 (cf. already 248). Cf. further Harrington
1992, 67; Theißen 2002, 339–40 (and 332–33n33).

[226] E.g., Davies 1977–78, 17. Käsemann, 1980, 293–94, interprets v. 14
against the background of a Jewish respectively apocalyptic vision of the future.
He thinks that "some of them" actually indicates "the whole of Israel." Against
such an undestanding, see Johnson 1984, 97–98.

[227] Theißen 2002, 340n42: "Schon in Röm 11,15 hatte Paulus betont, dass
die endzeitliche 'Annahme' Israels durch Gott 'Totenauferstehung' sei (und
nicht nur 'wie' eine Totenauferstehung). Das weist auf ein Wunder jenseits der
Geschichte."

[228] Ibid., 339–40: "Der Widerstand Israels gegen die Heidenmission war ja für Paulus die eigentliche Verblendung und 'Sünde' Israels (vgl. 1 Thess 2,14–16). Sie wäre definitiv überholt, wenn die Vollzahl der Heiden zum Heil gekommen ist."

[229] See below.

[230] Hofius 1989b, 197–98. He concludes, "*Israel kommt auf die gleiche Weise zum Glauben wie Paulus selbst!*" (198). Similarly, see Theißen 2002, 339: "So wie Paulus als ungläubiger Israelit durch eine Erscheinung vom Himmel bekehrt wurde, so wird auch ganz Israel durch den zur Parusie kommenden Christus gerettet werden." See also Longenecker 1989, 101: "Paul has simply transplanted this event from his own experience to the culmination point of the history of unbelieving Israel." Cf. Davies 1977–78, 34: "For him [Paul], there is no 'solution' to the Jewish question until we are at the very limit of history and at the threshold of the age to come, when God will be all in all and the distinctions of this world even between Jew and Gentile transcended." In a different context, he stresses the verb's passive form (*passivum divinum*) in the statement "The whole of Israel will be saved" (v. 26a) and maintains rightly that it points to "an activity of God whereby he will bring his covenant [. . .] to fruition." Against, see Räisänen 1987, 2918–19.

[231] Cf. Sänger 1986, 109: "Über den Modus, *wie* das geschehen soll und darüber, *was* dies Geschehen impliziert, äußert sich der Apostel an diesem Punkt nicht. Jedoch deutet er zumindest an, daß Israels jetzige Situation keineswegs als ein unveränderlicher status quo festgeschrieben ist." See also 117. Similarly, see Walter 1984, 177: "Es *bleibt* vielmehr Gottes Geheimnis, *wie* er das bewerkstelligen wird, was Paulus von ihm mit Gewißheit erwartet." Here, it remains unanswered "wie sich die erhoffte Erlösung dieses (und nur dieses einen) Volkes zu dem Individualprinzip des Heils verhält" (ibid.). See further Brandenburger 1985, 46; Harrington 1992, 61, 66–67.

[232] Shum 2002, 236–40. Cf. Koch 1986, 175–78; Lübking 1986, 124–25.

[233] For similarities between Ps. 50:2 and Isa. 59:19–20, see Hofius 1989b, 196n82. Here I intentionally pass on the question of an eventual text-critical conjecture in LXX Isa. 59:20. See Schaller 1984.

[234] Cf. Cranfield 1981, 577; Schreiner 1998, 619.

[235] Cf. Wagner 2003, 284–86.

[236] Cranfield 1981, 578; Dunn 1988, 682; Hvalvik 1990, 92; Legarth 2004, 257–59; Schreiner 1998, 619–20. *Pace* Shum 2002, 243–44, 247.

[237] E.g., Davies 1977–78, 27. Otherwise, see Hvalvik 1990, 92. At least one rabbinic text (BT Sanh. 98a) interprets Isa. 59:20 as referring to the Messiah. See Harrington 1992, 62. However, he is uncertain whether the Old Testament quotation relates to God or Christ (61–63).

[238] *Pace* Räisänen 1987, 2920. Here, he claims a little surprisingly (in contrast to the apparent eschatological context) that "das Futur in 11,26b

kontextbedingt ist und das Anvisierte vom Gesichtspunkt des alttestamentlichen Propheten (nicht aber von dem des Paulus) aus als zukünftig bezeichnet."
Similarly, see Hvalvik 1990, 93.

[239] Cf. especially Hofius 1989b, 196. "Die Angabe, daß der ῥυόμενος 'aus
Zion' kommen wird, muß nicht notwendig auf das Erscheinen Christi vom
himmlischen Jerusalem her gedeutet werden. Paulus kann sehr wohl an den
irdischen Zion denken, auf dem sich Christus bei der Parusie offenbaren
und von dem aus er sein Rettungswerk an Israel vollführen wird." Neither is
it necessary to interpret Rom. 11:26b–27 as a critique of the Old Testament's
notion of the eschatological pilgrimage of the Gentiles to Jerusalem that
ought to introduce the end times (see, e.g., Isa. 2:2ff.; Mic. 4:1ff.). Would Paul
have modified the tradition and meant that such prophecies are *already now*
fulfilled in a different manner through faith in the gospel? Then he would
have emphasized that only after this event the Jews themselves would flow
into the Christian church! Cf. Hübner in reference to many others: "Anstelle
der Wallfahrt der Völker die 'Wallfahrt' der Schätze der Heiden (Jes 60,1 ff.,
vor allem 60,5 f.), sprich: die paulinische Kollekte, geschehen wird" (1984,
112). Similarly, see, e.g., Lübking 1986, 124–25. Although the apostle surely
reserves his freedom to make new spiritual interpretations, they need not
completely and wholly exclude a literal fulfillment of the Old Testament
statements. He may well have thought that the Gentiles would go up to Zion
in connection to the conversion of Israel as stated in Rom. 11:26b–27. Cf.
further Theißen 2002, 339n41: "Man muss hier also nicht unbedingt an das
himmlische Jerusalem denken. Dass der zur Parusie kommende Christus
vom Himmel kommt, ist ohnehin selbstverständlich." See also Walter 1984,
182.

[240] Hvalvik 1990, 96. Cf. also Müller 1964, 46, 106–8.

[241] Then Israel finally follows in Abraham's footsteps and, like him, believes
in God, who makes the ungodly righteous by his grace alone (Rom. 4; see
above).

[242] Schreiner 1998, 619–20.

[243] Piper 1993, 25–31. Against, see Räisänen 1987, especially 2930–36. His
argumentation has been criticized by Schreiner 1998, 621–23. See also Spanje
1999. First he refers to Räisänen's arguments (91–119) and then transitions to
a thorough assessment of them (139–253). Cf. Brandenburger 1985, 43–47;
Lübking 1986, 99ff., 135ff. Against, see also Theißen 2002, 322, and many
others.

[244] Walter 1984, 176–77.

[245] For sure, it should not be forgotten that the initial pericope, which consists of a complaint against Israel, finishes with a eulogy in 9:5. See section
"(1) Prologue" above.

[246] Dunn 1988, 698. See also Jeremias 1977, 203–4.

²⁴⁷ Moo 1996, 741–42. Jeremias also thinks that "judgments" points to "das Richtende" and "ways" to "das rettende Heilshandeln" (1977, 204).

²⁴⁸ For Rom. 1:2–4 and 16:25–26, see Laato 2006, 47–50; above section "D. Bonhoeffer's Attempt to Solve the Hermeneutic Dilemma," chapter 3.

²⁴⁹ Theißen tries to explain God's "completely irrational" election by drawing attention to its obvious conditions: "Der erwählte und berufene Teil Israels war immer der schwächere: Isaak wurde von überalterten Eltern geboren, Jakob war der Jüngere, Mose vertrat gegenüber dem Pharao die versklavten Israeliten. Mit dieser Vorzugswahl der Schwächeren aber ist eine Verheißung verbunden: Sobald (das ungläubige) Israel in die Rolle des Geringeren und Schwächeren eintritt, könnte es eine erneute Chance haben" (2002, 322). But in essence, God's election can never be explained, only praised!

²⁵⁰ See, e.g., Dunn 1988, 698; Jeremias 1977, 204; Koch 1986, 178–79. Cf. further Moo 1996, 743. He tries to equate the three questions (vv. 34–35) with the three previous assertions:

a. "Who has known the mind of the Lord?" (v. 34 a) corresponds to the expression of God's inscrutable ways (v. 33c).
b. "Who has been his counselor?" (v. 34b) coincides with the utterance of God's unsearchable judgments (v. 33b).
c. "Who has given a gift to him that he might be repaid?" repeats the statement concerning the depth of the riches and wisdom and knowledge of God, whose characteristics point to his mercy (v. 33a).

²⁵¹ Obviously, Paul translates Job 41:2 directly from the Hebrew. His other citation of Job's book (1 Cor. 3:19) also differentiates itself from LXX! See especially Koch 1986, 72–73. Cf. Hübner 1984, 126.

²⁵² The statement "from him and through him and to him are all things" in v. 36 has various occasional parallels in Stoicism but should be perceived against the Pauline theological background. Cf. Cranfield 1981, 591: "But the sense of the formula as used by Paul is far from the pantheism of the Stoic use of it." Similarly, see Moo 1996, 743: "Hellenistic Jews picked up this language and applied it to Yahweh; and it is probably, therefore, from the synagogue that Paul borrows this formula."

²⁵³ Hübner 1984, 126. Cf. further Dunn 1988, 704: "In an argument which began with man's rebellion against God as creator (1:18–25), what could be more appropriate than a final acclamation of God the creator?" Similarly, see already Jeremias 1977, 203, with the following summary of the line of thought in Romans: "Damit schließt sich ein Ring: die Preisgabe der Heiden, von der Röm 1, 24. 26. 28 die Rede war und die 11, 32 a auf Israel ausgedehnt ist, wird aufgehoben durch die Grenzenlosigkeit des göttlichen Erbarmens."

[254] For the Pauline theology in general, see Jeremias 1977, 205: "Immer wieder beobachten wir, daß sein Ringen und Fragen nicht eher zur Ruhe kommt, als bis es zur δόξα Gottes gefunden hat."

[255] See Laato 2009a, 216–18. Cf. Westerholm 2004b, 437–38.

[256] See, above all, Odland 1937, 91. Later on, see also Thurén 1994, 250–52.

[257] First Corinthians 13:4–7 personify ἀγάπη directly with Christ. It is seen most deeply in *his* characteristics that are described there!

[258] Cf. Thurén 1994, 250.

[259] Cf. Moo 1996, 663n11. He maintains that the verb *hear* in 10:14 "normally takes the genitive to denote the person who is heard (as opposed to the thing that is heard, which is usually denoted with the accusative). [. . .] Therefore Paul may use the genitive to suggest that Christ is the one who is heard in the message of the gospel."

[260] Silva 1993, 639.

[261] Wagner 2003, 356–57. Similarly, see Shum 2002, 247: "Our examination of the Isaianic material in Rom.9–11 has shown that Paul's appropriation of the material exhibits a very strong theological continuity between its original and its new contexts." See also Wilk 1998, 265: "Das zentrale Ergebnis der vorstehenden Analysen lautet: Paulus führt Jesajazitate niemals ohne gleichzeitige Bezüge auf den jeweiligen Kontext an; in aller Regel spiegelt das paulinische Umfeld diesen Kontext mehrfach wieder."

[262] Cf., however, the warning in *Att tolka bibeln i dag* 1995, 58: "Den bokstavliga meningen får inte förväxlas med den bokstavliga mening eller 'bokstavstrogna' bibeltolkning som fundamentalister talar om." See also 60–61.

[263] The hard-to-comprehend concept *sensus plenior* is used here in accordance with the Christological perspective such as it appears in this work. For other definitions, see Moo 1986, 201–4, 209–11. He combines a deeper meaning in the Old Testament text with "a canonical approach" (204–9) that also involves a strong Christological interpretation: "The New Testament views the Old Testament as a collection of books that, in each of its parts and in its whole, was somehow 'incomplete' until 'filled up' through the advent of Christ and the inauguration of the era of salvation." See above. Modern Catholicism presents a different definition of *sensus plenior*. See, e.g., *Att tolka bibeln i dag* 1995, 62. Contrary to a number of Roman Catholic scholars who emphasize traditions of the church fathers and the church, Longenecker 1999 underscores, "Protestant proponents, who hold a *sola Scriptura* doctrine, confine a *sensus plenior* to the New Testament" (xxxii). Notice further Brown 1955.

[264] All in all, the concept of hermeneutics should in this work not be misunderstood as a euphemism for "the skill of all but totally ignoring the Bible while appearing to accept it" (Silva 1992, 156)!

V. Summary and Conclusions

[1] Cf., e.g., Evans 1984, 570: "Paul's vision of God [= his conversion] became the basis of his hermeneutic, that is, how he must interpret history (the present) and sacred tradition (the past)."

[2] Cf. here Moo 1986, 210: "Many apparently 'new' meanings discovered in Old Testament texts by New Testament authors are no more than the literal sense of those passages when read against the 'informing' theology that precedes them."

[3] Cf. the argumentation in Jeanrond 1991. He argues for a completely new combination of hermeneutics and action for the theological discipline: "What we are looking for here is a mode of thinking that allows for a dialectical relationship between theories of biblical interpretation and theories of Christian action, that is, a speculative framework in which the different theoretical tasks of theology are united once again."

[4] Moo 1986, 185, rightly argues that "the New Testament appeal to the Old Testament is too basic to the church's very identity to leave it in the realm of unexplained assertion."

[5] Cf. especially Vanhoozer 1998. He does, in fact, only speak about the author, the reader, and the text, but the message is included in the term *text* (as the title of the book reveals).

[6] Vanhoozer's starting point is the trinity as a hermeneutic key, which is especially seen in the second part of the book: "In Part 2 I will explore the parallels between three sets of triads: Father, Son, and Spirit; author, text, and reader; metaphysics, epistemology, and ethics" (1998, 189n64). His method has, without a doubt, many relevant aspects. Still, he should have taken a deeper look into the biblical texts to show that his hermeneutic approach and conclusions are first and foremost built on them. It is not uncommon that aspects, belonging to systematic theology and being central or relevant in themselves, become loose principles that lack biblical anchoring or application. It still remains for Vanhoozer to prove that his deep argumentation truly is in accordance with Holy Scripture. Otherwise, he will easily get adrift in the future. The best scenario is that exegesis supports the position (in this case, the trinitarian hermeneutic structure) that dogmatics represent.

[7] Cf. Sasse 1981, 244: "Die Wahrheit ist nicht die Summe der Wahrheiten. Sie ist nicht ein System von Sätzen. Das ist der Wahrheitsbegriff der Philosophie, der seit den Apologeten des 2. Jahrhunderts immer wieder in die Kirche eingedrungen ist. Was Wahrheit im Sinne des Neuen Testaments, im Sinne der ganzen Bibel ist, das kann nur der verstehen, der den sonderbarsten und größten Satz verstanden hat, der jemals auf Erden über die Wahrheit gesagt worden ist: 'Ich bin die Wahrheit!'"

[8] For the canon process and canon criteria, see, e.g., Carson—Moo—Morris 1992, 487–500; especially Bokedal 2005. Cf. Ellis 1991, 3–50. According to

latest research, the enumerated criteria supposedly testify about an attempt to motivate the formation of canon *after* the fact. See mainly Ludlow 2003, 69–93. She argues: "Rather, there is some sense in which the canon chose (or formed) the Church, rather than the Church chose (or formed) the canon. For this reason, then, the whole practice of talking about *criteria* of canonicity is called into question, for what seems to be happening—at least in part—is that the Church is formulating *reasons* or *explanations* for why it has what it has, not *criteria* for choosing what it should have in the future" (70–71). In reference to her, see, e.g., Veijola 2004, 64–65. In any case, the "interpreted" canon process shows under such circumstances considerable and obvious similarities with the hermeneutics of Romans. Cf. Ludlow 2003, 71: "Whereas it may be impossible to reconstruct the precise history of how the canon came to be, it is possible—and perhaps equally instructive—to give an account of early Church views on the nature of what was going on."

⁹ See especially Ludlow 2003, 71: "In particular, I want to argue that a study of the early Church's reflection on the canonical books shows that one needs to keep in balance *both* the Church's passive reception *and* its active creation of the canon of Scripture—however paradoxical that may sound." Cf. further 72: "Thus, the very thing which seems to be a source of frustration to some historians of the formation of the canon—that one cannot draw up a neat list of 'canonical criteria'—becomes key to an understanding of the canon's formation."

¹⁰ Here I refer to a personal discussion with prof. Gordon Wenham during European Theological Students' Conference in Mittersill (August 4–11, 2001). See also Carson 1986, 6. Cf. further Linnemann 1990, 137–41.